Your Role as General Counsel

How to Survive and Thrive in Your Role as GC

Authors
Ian White and Simon McCall

Managing director
Sian O'Neill

Your Role as General Counsel: How to Survive and Thrive in Your Role as GC
is published by

Globe Law and Business Ltd
3 Mylor Close
Horsell
Woking
Surrey GU21 4DD
United Kingdom
Tel: +44 20 3745 4770
www.globelawandbusiness.com

Printed and bound in Great Britain by Severn, Gloucester

Your Role as General Counsel: How to Survive and Thrive in Your Role as GC

ISBN 9781787424029
EPUB ISBN 9781787424036
Adobe PDF ISBN 9781787424043
Mobi ISBN 9781787424050

Table of contents

Acknowledgements

This Special Report could not have been written without the help of so many people. First and foremost, we would like to thank our wonderful publishers, Sian O'Neill and Katerina Menhennet, who encouraged us throughout the journey, were patient with us when they must have been frustrated, and were full of good ideas, tips and insights. Without them, the report would have had little chance of ever seeing the light of day. We would also like to thank our colleagues at Sherwood PSF Consulting, not least for their insights on effective coaching.

Ian would like to thank the following – friends as well as colleagues:

- Paul Gilbert, for kindly suggesting us to Sian in the first place, but also for his insight on the role of the effective general counsel (GC). I, like so many others, have much to thank Paul for: friend, colleague, collaborator, wise counsel in every sense of that word, and occasional breakfast and drinking buddy (though never together!);
- Simon Cox and Claire Carless, for their guidance on how to play the role of GC as well as what to do afterwards;
- Louisa Elder, for sharing her experiences of transition from a legal career to many different careers;
- Brian Littleton, for his sterling career advice; and
- Martin Spencer, for his ever-wise and thoughtful advice on how to work and live successfully in whatever role you take on.

Simon would like to thank:

- Philip Tranter, a long-time business contact, friend and (now) music quiz team-mate, for his interesting insights on life as an in-house lawyer; and
- my Sherwood friends and colleagues (former and current), who have contributed so many of the ideas that appear in this report as result of our work together on consultancy assignments and development programmes over the last 21 years – Des O'Connell, Gwyn Price, Chris Stoakes, Julian Boardman-Weston, Sally Woodward, Jo Minns and Chris Hadfield.

I. Introduction – why you need this Special Report

Consigliere of mine, I think you should tell your Don what everyone seems to know!
Don Corleone, *The Godfather*[1]

1. Who has this Special Report been written for?

When we first thought about writing a report for general counsel (GCs), part of the reasoning was how useful it would have been to have had all the knowledge, wisdom and skills needed to embark on the GC journey when we started our own careers in-house. While it might not necessarily have fallen under Don Corleone's description, a guide on what to know – or at least, get to know – to undertake the role successfully would have been invaluable. Alas, nothing was available then; but hopefully, today this report will fill the gap.

Although this report is primarily intended as a practical guide for GCs and perhaps aspiring GCs – a well-thumbed tome that we hope will assist you both day to day and over the longer term – we believe that it will also be a useful reference for many others, including:

- lawyers starting off in their first in-house role;
- those new to a particular sector or business; and
- those contemplating a move in-house away from the constraints

of private practice and perhaps considering a more business-oriented role.

It might also be of use to business people generally: CEOs, CFOs, HR directors and others who come into regular contact with the GC and the legal team. One thing we often encounter in our work is GCs complaining that the CEO and other leaders don't 'get' legal or what it does, so having a report that explains some of the background may help. In addition, many of these people will be involved in recruiting or managing the legal team, so we have focused on this too.

2. How this Special Report is set out

The first thing to say is that throughout this report, we ask lots of questions that we think you will want to answer. Accordingly, we would hope that a well-used copy will have a combination of scribbles down the margins and notes tucked between the pages. We would like this to be a 'workbook', not just a 'reading book'. Also at the back of the report, we have included some notes pages, where you can jot down key words and themes from your reading which may occur to you as you go along, together with any relevant thoughts you might have. We discovered this idea in Brene Brown's book *The Gifts of Imperfection*[2] and believe that it can help you to coordinate your ideas as you go along.

In Chapter II, we ask: what type of GC are you? Or: what type of GC do you want to be? This will depend to some extent on the hand you have been dealt. Joining a company as its first in-house lawyer will be a very different experience from running a team of 50 lawyers and having more resources at your disposal. If you are establishing a legal function, you might have a lot of latitude and be able to shape your own role and that of your department. If there is already a legal department, you will need to ask yourself some questions. What are they like? Are they effective? What do you need to do to make them effective? You may be taking over a very slick team and may thus be tempted to leave things as they are. Alternatively, you might have been 'parachuted in' to revitalise a demoralised legal department with a poor reputation. These are all very different scenarios and your approach to each will be different – though there may be common themes too.

In Chapter III, we look at your first 100 days. Understanding the organisation and making the right impression are key if you are going to survive and succeed; so here we consider how best to do so. What due diligence should you do before you start? What is the best way to approach the role when you begin? What will success look like? How would you like to be able to describe to a friend or colleague how your first 100 days went? What went well and what went not so well during those 100 days? What would you do differently if you had them again? The first 100 days are crucial in establishing your credibility, so it is important that you plan for them and deliver accordingly. You might only aspire to run the legal department well and ensure that your employer complies with its legal duties. Or you might see yourself as a close adviser to the board and the executive committee (exco). You might even see yourself as a *consigliere* to the CEO and their team. Which will it be? Or could it be?

Developing a strategy for the legal team is the focus of Chapter IV (and is revisited from a different perspective in Chapter V). We look at the information that you will need and the factors that you should take into account. We suggest that you encapsulate your strategy in a way that would pass the 'elevator test'.

In Chapter V, we examine how to manage your in-house legal department as a business unit in its own right. To do this, we run through the typical business function headings – finance, marketing, HR, learning and development (L&D) and (briefly) operations.

Chapter VI explores how you can best build your team – and again,

"The first 100 days are crucial in establishing your credibility, so it is important that you plan for them and deliver accordingly."

considers how you will determine the role and purpose of the in-house function.

How to be a coach and/or mentor to your team is the subject of Chapter VII. Are you already a coach? If not, now might be the time to develop your coaching skills! Or are you a mentor? What's the difference between the two? And is it important? Ultimately, you will need to guide and develop your team if both you and they are to succeed. Who can help with this – both internally and outside of the organisation?

Your relationship with the board will also be vital. We look at this in Chapter VIII. Boards can be tricky for advisers to manoeuvre around – particularly if they are unitary in nature, with both executives and non-executives, creating potential conflicts for the unwary. What exposure to the board do you need? What exposure to the board are you likely to have?

In Chapter IX, we consider whether GCs should take on the role of company secretary, either alongside their existing duties or as a separate role. While many GCs see the company secretary position as an add-on, it is very much a role in its own right – and one that requires very different skills and qualities from those of the GC. So beware!

Finally, in Chapter X, we consider other career possibilities beyond the confines of a purely legal role, remembering that in this ever-changing world, there is a need to reinvent yourself regularly.

To help guide you on your way, we have included a number of case studies and interviews that draw on the insight and experience of a number of seasoned practitioners. We have also highlighted models and guidance produced by others which we believe will be of further help.

We hope that this is useful, along with the report generally – but only you can be the judge of that!

II. Legal *consigliere* or functional manager?

1. Introduction

Those of you who, like us, are Stieg Larsson fans may recall the final book in the Millennium Series – *The Girl in the Spider's Web*. That book contains the immortal lines: "What I actually said was that all you needed was a gang of lawyers... Lawyers are the hitmen of our times."[3]

We are pretty sure that if you asked most CEOs what they looked for in their GC, they wouldn't say, "We want a hit man! Or hit woman!" But how many of them would be able to define what they really expected or wanted from their GC? Unlike a role such as HR director, being a GC can mean many different things to both lawyers and others. So perhaps the first thing that you need to ask when you accept the position is: what type of GC is your new employer looking for? Or, if you would like more control: what sort of GC do you aspire to be? Answering this question early on can be fundamental to your success.

As a starting point, have a conversation with your CEO about what they are expecting from you in your role. We commonly hear GCs complaining that their CEO doesn't 'get them' and hasn't bothered to find out what they do or what their role entails. Comments like these always amaze us! GCs like these are unlikely to have an easy time in their role. CEOs are busy people who will rarely come around to talk to the GC about their role and what it entails (though some might). You need to be proactive here and talk regularly with your CEO to understand clearly what the mandate is and what the CEO, the board and the management team are expecting. And you should regularly review this too – perhaps a couple of times a year. Companies, dynamics and people all change – and your role will too. One of us wishes that he had communicated with his CEOs more openly and extensively, especially when things weren't going well (rather than sidling away and expressing exactly what he thought of the CEO in a string of expletives!). Building an effective relationship with your CEO will be critical to your success – and maybe even survival – in your role.

Tips: GC's mandate and lines of communication

- Review the GC's mandate and that of the legal team every six months or so. Is it still fit for purpose or does it need revising to fit in with the changing needs of the organisation? Perhaps discuss this first with the HR director and then the CEO. Amend the mandate as appropriate.
- Ensure that you have a clear line of communication with the CEO – and not just in times of trouble. Spend time working on and developing the relationship. This is especially important if you do not have a direct reporting line to the CEO.

While GCs come in all shapes and sizes, we have broadly divided them into two categories: functional managers and legal *consiglieri*. Let's look at both of these in turn.

2. Functional managers

In some companies, the role of the GC – or perhaps more accurately, head of legal – is seen very much as a support role, helping to steer the business out of trouble, providing legal advice, reviewing contracts and so on. You will be responsible for ensuring that the organisation stays on the right side of the law, with legal and regulatory responsibilities ranging from companies law to competition regulation and health and safety legislation. It is unlikely that you will sit on the exco; but then, we do not believe that the GC necessarily needs to – and from an independence perspective when advising the exco, it is often better if you don't. You will still be a respected member of the senior management team and a valued employee within the company.

3. Legal *consiglieri*

This, of course, is the more exciting role; but not every company wants one and not every GC aspires to this. And, of course, we are not suggesting that you take on the role like Tom Hagan did in *The Godfather*! However, this is the type of role that many GCs do want to fulfil – and over time, many can. It is often described as being a 'trusted adviser' to the board and management team, but we think

"Building an effective relationship with your CEO will be critical to your success – and maybe even survival – in your role."

this is a bit over-simplistic: if a GC can't be trusted and is not seen as an 'adviser', then what exactly are they? It should go without saying that a GC is a trusted adviser.

So what does the role of legal *consigliere* entail? Apart from handling all the 'routine' matters – such as dealing with external lawyers, legal costs, regulatory and compliance relationships – a legal *consigliere* is someone whom the CEO and executive team can fully involve in the running of the business. In an excellent paper entitled *Do You Have the Right C-Suite?*, executive search firm Heidrick & Struggles describes the role as follows: "the GC should be able to work collaboratively with the senior executive team to achieve business goals – thinking like principal, not an agent, as outside counsel might – and contribute to company success both as a technical legal expert and a business generalist."[4]

Contributions to the business and to business decision making are key; this is why we often advise in-house lawyers early on in their careers to think of themselves as business people first and lawyers second. In the *consigliere* role, the GC acts as a sounding board to the CEO; challenges – albeit constructively – the ideas proposed by the board and the exco; and may possibly act as the right-hand person of the CEO. The GC is thus very much a business person first. However, this does not detract from the fact that, in our view, the GC should principally remain an adviser rather than a decision maker. And while it is useful for the GC to sense check others outside their immediate area of remit, it is important that the GC remains a lawyer. We once heard a GC who was a member of the exco complain that his CEO did not see him as someone who should advise on strategy and did not bring him into strategic discussions. "I am quite capable of advising on strategy," he said bitterly. Well, quite possibly; but then, quite possibly not. In any case, however, that is not the point. You don't hire the head of strategy to run the legal function; nor should the GC be responsible for other functional areas unless they have the ability to run them (and if they do, they probably shouldn't be running legal!) No, the GC as *consigliere* is there to help the team as a whole, not to run different functions.

There can, of course, be frustrations. One person we spoke to had advised a client while in private practice and, over time, had become trusted for his strategic and business advice. He moved in-house expecting this strategic and business role to develop; but in fact, he gradually found himself being drawn back into mainly legal work. This was important and valuable for the business, but was not quite his personal plan.

"The key is to be able to use a variety of resources and insights to ensure that the board, senior management and the company as a whole are fully aware of and can deal effectively with business issues."

The role of legal *consigliere* is challenging, but ultimately (more) rewarding. As the Heidrick & Struggles report concludes:

> *For the General Counsel, who must have a strong working relationship with the CEO but whose client is ultimately the company, these new expectations require a delicate balancing act as well as a wide range of leadership abilities. But if the position has become more demanding, it has also become more interesting to the best and the brightest legal practitioners.*[5]

These are sentiments that we would endorse.

So perhaps a good and effective GC needn't be a hitman or hitwoman after all. The key is to be able to use a variety of resources and insights to ensure that the board, senior management and the company as a whole are fully aware of and can deal effectively with business issues.

Interview with Simon Cox, GC of BBOXX

Simon Cox moved in-house at the relatively late age of 54, having previously been a partner at two well-known law firms. In his role at BBOXX – a private equity-backed company that provides energy solutions in the developing world – Simon is GC as well as heading HR and compliance.

Why did you move in-house?

A client poached me at the age of 54! I'm glad I did – I am a company/commercial lawyer who enjoys transactions and business. I also think that when you reach a certain age in a law firm, there is pressure from the others coming up. My boss now is 32 and I find that invigorating. You also need to enjoy the job and the company.

What would your advice be to someone moving in-house?

First, you need a bit of luck – having a client who wants you really helps. And depending on your seniority in private practice, you may have to take a salary cut. But I have joined a company that's going places and I relish that.

Second, in your management role, don't stick to the legal stuff and make sure you challenge to add value.

What would your advice be on the first 100 days in-house?

I was previously the external adviser to the company I joined, so I was already well embedded and had a greater understanding of the business. You must quickly get to know the business and the big issues. Listening skills are key. This means that you shouldn't rush into the role – don't do anything drastic or make big decisions. Keep close to the CEO and their priorities. Get the CEO to approve your priorities too. It is important, if you can, to report to the CEO and have a daily call with them. Of course, other people have to wait, which you will need to manage. Make sure you are visible.

And if you are starting a legal function...?
Make sure you have the right resources, infrastructure and budget; and be prepared to roll up your sleeves.

What would your advice be when it comes to taking on other roles?
That's fine, but you need subject-matter experts supporting you.

What would your advice be to the young Simon Cox?

- Have a good financial understanding – the more you understand here, the better.
- Public speaking – get better at it and be confident.
- Understand people – have a basic understanding of psychometrics.

III. The first 100 days

1. Creating a sense of success

Imagine that it's Day 101 since you took on your new role. You're having a conversation with someone who is interested to know how your first 100 days have gone. Now imagine that your (short) answer is, "Great! It's gone really well." You then go on to explain in more detail how and why "it's gone really well"; this will involve a mix of things that you would have confidently expected and some things that you would have been hopeful, but less certain, about. We're in Donald Rumsfeld territory here: there will be 'known knowns', 'known unknowns' and the mysterious 'unknown unknowns'.

However, we believe that from an early stage (which could include before you start the role), you can begin to build a picture of what success over your first 100 days could look, sound and feel like. You can use all your senses to create this picture:

- What would you like to hear (eg, warm, enthusiastic voices; thanks or praise; casual chats)?
- What would you like to see (eg, smiles and nods of recognition; engaged and attentive people around a meeting table)?
- How would you like to feel physically (eg, energetic; tension free; well rested)?
- How would you like to feel emotionally (eg, calm; excited; interested; balanced)?

Build your own picture of what you would like to hear, see and feel. Be as specific as possible. This process of creating a 'memory of the future' – termed 'scenario planning' – will increase the chances of your hopes becoming a reality.[6]

You will also have a list of tasks and accomplishments that you will want to tick off, such as:

- meeting your team;
- meeting key colleagues;
- reviewing (or starting to create) the strategy for the legal team;
- assessing the team's workload and work types; and
- reviewing and building relationships with key external lawyers.

Once again, continue to build your own list. (We will shortly provide a framework that may help here; but start with your own ideas.) We do suggest, however, that you also apply the scenario planning technique mentioned above to imagine what it will be like when you complete those tasks.

"Build your own picture of what you would like to hear, see and feel. Be as specific as possible. This process of creating a 'memory of the future' – termed 'scenario planning' – will increase the chances of your hopes becoming a reality."

2. Ways to generate ideas about a successful first 100 days

2.1 Who is interested?

One way to generate ideas about what a successful first 100 days could look like is to imagine the different people who might ask you: "How's it going in your new role?" The different perspectives and motivations of different people, including the following, may help you to generate a range of positive answers:

- your boss/direct report (eg, CEO, finance director, global GC);
- the person who hired you (if different);
- a fellow senior executive in the organisation (eg, COO, financial director, HR director);
- a member of your legal team;
- an external lawyer who knows your organisation well; and
- a spouse/partner/good friend (who is interested in your wellbeing, not just career success).

Add other people to this list who you can imagine having the same conversation with and who you would like to tell that things are going well. What might you say to them?

2.2 What hand have you been dealt?

A second approach is to use the well-known McKinsey 7-S Framework.[7] You can apply this to the legal department itself (if it is of sufficient size or complexity to warrant this approach), and/or to the business or organisation as a whole, to gain a comprehensive and balanced overview of the organisation (or part of it) and how it works.

Structure

Strategy *Systems*

Shared values

Staff *Skills*

Style

The elements basically speak for themselves. There are three 'hard' Ss:

- Structure: How is the team/business structured? What does (or would) the organisational chart show?
- Strategy: What are the objectives and goals of the team/business? How does it plan to achieve them?
- Systems: What are the key processes that enable the team/business to operate effectively and efficiently?

The three 'soft' Ss are as follows:

- Staff: What people do you have?
- Skills: What skills (technical, management, personal) do they have? What skills are needed?
- Style: What is the look and feel of the team/organisation (eg, formal/informal – in terms of dress sense, hierarchy and how people talk to each other)?

Sitting in the middle are the critical 'shared values' – which are different from and more important than 'style'. These are the key cultural norms: what really matters in and to the organisation (eg, making money; contributing to society; being innovative; being respected)? What is it that gets people praised and promoted? What is it that the organisation wants to see about itself in the media? (This is likely to be an organisation-wide issue. It's unlikely, but not impossible, that the legal team will have fundamentally different shared values from the rest of the organisation.)

To gather information about the legal team or the organisation as a whole, we suggest that you look at both formal and informal sources:

- Formal sources include annual reports, strategy papers, operational reviews, appraisal reports and corporate social media; and
- Informal sources include conversations inside and outside the office, individual social media, organisation social events and – something that we think can be really valuable – stories that have become part of the folklore of the organisation. Listen out for "Everyone remembers the time when..." and "We all thought X was a legend here because...". These stories can be particularly helpful in getting a sense of the shared values of the organisation.

3. Credibility, rapport and trust

During your first 100 days, you will want to establish and build relationships with colleagues. This can be at both a business and a personal level. You will know from past experience how important it is to work with people who 'get you' and respect you. This doesn't mean trying to be best friends with everyone. It does mean giving yourself the advantage of being regarded positively – which will help you to get things done.

(An aside here, in case you are reading this section and thinking, "But the people at my new organisation already know me": we know of many GCs – some of whom we interviewed for this Special Report – who have moved in-house to businesses that were previously their

"Listen out for 'Everyone remembers the time when...' and 'We all thought X was a legend here because...'. These stories can be particularly helpful in getting a sense of the shared values of the organisation."

clients in private practice. In that case, yes, the CEO and maybe others know you; but do you want to them to see you in the same light now that you are part of the business, as opposed to an external adviser sending in invoices? How about people who don't know you? We think that the idea of planning your first 100 days and using the ideas outlined in this chapter is still relevant.)

One way to cultivate these relationships is by developing three positive and powerful attributes: credibility, rapport and trust. These are probably generated in that order, although of course they interlink and are mutually supportive.

3.1 Credibility

To put it simply, people appreciate that you 'know your stuff' – that you have valuable experience and expertise.

The first important point here is to remember that you will probably arrive in the role with a certain amount (very likely, a great deal) of credibility. You may have previously been a partner in a highly regarded law firm; you may have specific recognised legal skills; you may have sector-relevant knowledge. The people who recruited you will know this – and so will others if they have asked around or looked you up on LinkedIn.

You can further build up your credibility in your early days by:

- continuing your background research on the organisation (which you doubtless started as part of your application due diligence). It will give you confidence, and give other people confidence in you, to be able to say, "Ah yes, I read/heard/know about that...";
- showing yourself to be willing and open to listen and learn about the organisation when you can't say "I know about that ...";
- sharing appropriate anecdotes about your relevant experience (but beware of overdoing the "When I was at..." war stories);
- really taking on board communication (whether in conversation, email or other channels) when the person you are communicating with indicates that they regard it as important. (We will say something about the importance of listening shortly, but think about asking questions and recapping as a way to show that you are giving due attention to what they are saying or writing); and
- preparing carefully for meetings and important conversations.

3.2 Rapport

Building rapport involves wanting to understand other people, showing interest in them and seeing things from their perspective,

"Building credibility, rapport and trust is important not only in the first 100 days, but also if at any time you need to 'restart' – for example, with a change in role or a move to a different part of the organisation."

so that they realise you care. To some extent, it is developed through small talk by the coffee machine; but it can and should be much more than that. Other ways to build rapport include:

- conducting a bit of background research about the people in your legal team or key colleagues, so that you can say, "Ah yes, Alex, you're the keen walker/choir singer/Aston Villa supporter/ in the middle of your master's/part of the Project X team";
- listening out for and remembering the personal and business things that matter to different individuals, and asking to hear more about them; and
- noticing if someone looks particularly happy or a bit stressed, and showing an interest in their wellbeing.

We know of some people who can walk through a busy open-plan office and literally or figuratively put their head down and neither transmit any information to nor receive any information from the people in the room. Similarly, we know of people who instinctively (or with a bit of effort) look around and exchange a nod, a smile or a raise of the hand, or pause for a micro-conversation. It's pretty obvious which approach tends to build rapport. We would suggest that even quiet and shy people – not just loud, extrovert types – can adopt the 'rapport-friendly' approach described above.

3.3 Trust

The word really says it all. People trust you – they trust your opinions and judgements. They trust you to deliver on your promises. This almost inevitably takes time to develop. People decide to trust based on experience. Some ways to start building trust include:

- (obviously) doing what you say you will do;
- respecting confidential information that is shared with you;
- being prepared to explain your reasons for decisions; and
- treating colleagues with respect and care, both when you listen to them and when you talk to them.

Building credibility, rapport and trust is important not only in the first 100 days, but also if at any time you need to 'restart' – for example, with a change in role or a move to a different part of the organisation; or if a new CEO arrives and you need to start relationship building all over again.

4. Listening

As will probably have been apparent from what we have said so far, a lot of time during your first 100 days should be spent listening. You will be gathering information about people and the organisation from conversations with individuals, both informally and in meetings.

"A helpful way to think about listening is to check your intent. If your intent is to understand, then you are likely to listen well."

How well developed are your listening skills? Have you had feedback from others about this? When people have let you know that you listen well, have they explained why? What about if you have had negative feedback? Again, do you understand what you have been doing that causes people to think you could listen better? Think about and visualise the people you know who are very good listeners: what is it that they do differently?

A simple (albeit somewhat cheesy) mnemonic for good listening is EARS:

- **E**mpathise: Demonstrate to the other person that you are taking care to listen attentively. This can be done with simple nods, gestures and encouraging sounds – the opposite of a 'stony silence' or a 'blank stare'.
- **A**sk questions: If you can ask relevant and thoughtful questions, this will show that you have been listening carefully and enable you to clarify any uncertainties you may have.
- **R**ecap: The ability to recap and summarise what the other person says is an effective way of demonstrating that you are listening – for example, "Have I got this right – what you're saying is X, Y, Z?" And, of course, it's a good way to check that you have been understanding correctly.

- **S**ilence: A good way to listen is not to talk! If you are about to have a conversation where your main objective is to receive information, try thinking in advance, "I should only do 20% or 30% of the talking, so that most of the time I am listening."

A helpful way to think about listening is to check your intent. If your intent is to understand, then you are likely to listen well. Someone whose main intent is to respond will likely be working out what they want to say while the other person is still talking (and then possibly start to respond before the other person has finished their sentence). It's difficult to listen and rehearse a response at the same time. As someone once memorably put it, "In my business, people don't listen, they reload!"

Traffic-light planning process

As you go through your first 100 days, you will be thinking about and planning the actions that you want to take. Instinctively, you will be notetaking – whether that's mentally, digitally or in a notebook. The following traffic-light system is a good way to organise your thoughts and potential actions:

- **Red:** Things that are unhelpful and you are sure that your team should stop doing – for example, Monday morning meetings which you can see are not productive, an inefficient way of allocating work or a performance measure that encourages the wrong behaviour.
- **Orange:** Things that are working reasonably well, but may need reviewing and tweaking – for example, how outside lawyers are instructed and monitored, how knowledge management is handled or how the current flexible working policy is operating.
- **Green:** Things that need to start happening, but are not happening at the moment – for example, Monday morning team meetings to share information, briefings with other departments and teams within the business, or the introduction of a new reward structure.

IV. Developing a legal strategy

1. A preliminary comment about strategy

When talking about strategy (in any context), we would suggest that there are three elements to take into account before delving into the details of a strategic plan:

- **Values:** What values and culture underpin and guide the organisation?
- **Process:** How will the strategy be put together? Who will be involved – top down from the board – or, in our context, the GC – or bottom up, involving all staff? Considering and then communicating explicitly about process helps to manage expectations. It can be very frustrating for people at a senior level to carefully craft a sensible strategy, only for other people to fail to buy into it (even if they agree with the content of the strategy), because they were not consulted along the way.
- **Content:** What is in the strategy in terms of the objectives and the means of achieving those objectives?

2. Legal strategy

Developing a strategy for how the business or organisation as a whole addresses legal risks and issues is an important aspect of the job of a GC. It's obviously way beyond the day-to-day administration and management of the in-house legal department. It's also about more than creating a strategy for the in-house legal team alone.

There are two ways to approach this. The first is by looking at who is involved in work that has a direct or indirect legal impact on the business, such as:

- the in-house legal team;
- external lawyers in private practice law firms;
- people in the business whose roles have a legal impact – for example, in HR (dealing with employment issues), in procurement (dealing with commercial contracts) and in R&D (dealing with IP matters); and
- the board, taking important strategic decisions.

The first two groups are obvious; and it is equally clear that they need to adopt a consistent approach to the legal risks and activities that are of greatest importance to the business.

The next two groups are important for different reasons. It would likely be an operational nightmare if every time that someone in HR, procurement or R&D came across a legal issue, they stopped work, ran to the in-house legal team and waited for an answer. Equally, it would be alarming if they just ploughed on without any guidance. (We will look later at how that guidance could be given.)

On the other hand, one would definitely want the board to pause and consult before taking a decision with a major legal impact. That will happen (hopefully) if the GC is actually in the room or at the Zoom meeting. But what if they are not? In that situation, the board needs to have legal issues on its radar and understand the legal strategy for the business.

It's also helpful to recognise how legal risks (and opportunities) sit alongside other important risks that an organisation is likely to face. The relevance and priority of other risks are likely to vary by business and sector, but a generic list would include:

- strategic risk (getting major decisions wrong) (eg, launch/withdrawal of a product or service, or entry to/departure from the Indian market);
- financial risk (eg, cash-flow problems, capital investment mistakes or borrowing errors);
- operational risk (eg, being unable to manufacture goods because of labour problems or to provide a service because of regulatory action);
- reputational risk (eg, hitting the media with a bad news story or a casual, throwaway remark of the CEO that has backfired);
- IT and digital risk (eg, cybersecurity failures or privacy problems); and

- people risk (eg, losing a key team to a rival or failing to invest in L&D).

These types of risks inevitably overlap and interrelate – and this is particularly the case with legal risk. What are the legal risks of starting to do business in India? Or borrowing from a third-tier lender? Or putting the CEO in front of a tenacious journalist?

2.1 How to develop a legal strategy

Here is our suggested step-by-step approach to developing a legal strategy. Of course, it will need to be tailored to the particular circumstances of your business. If a legal strategy is already in place, it could serve as a checklist for reviewing it. (Alternatively, if you are reading this in advance of taking up a GC position, this could help to clarify the expected scope of the role during the selection process.)

The completed process can be seen in Figure 1 – and we will take you through it in stages.

Figure 1: Step-by-step approach to legal strategy

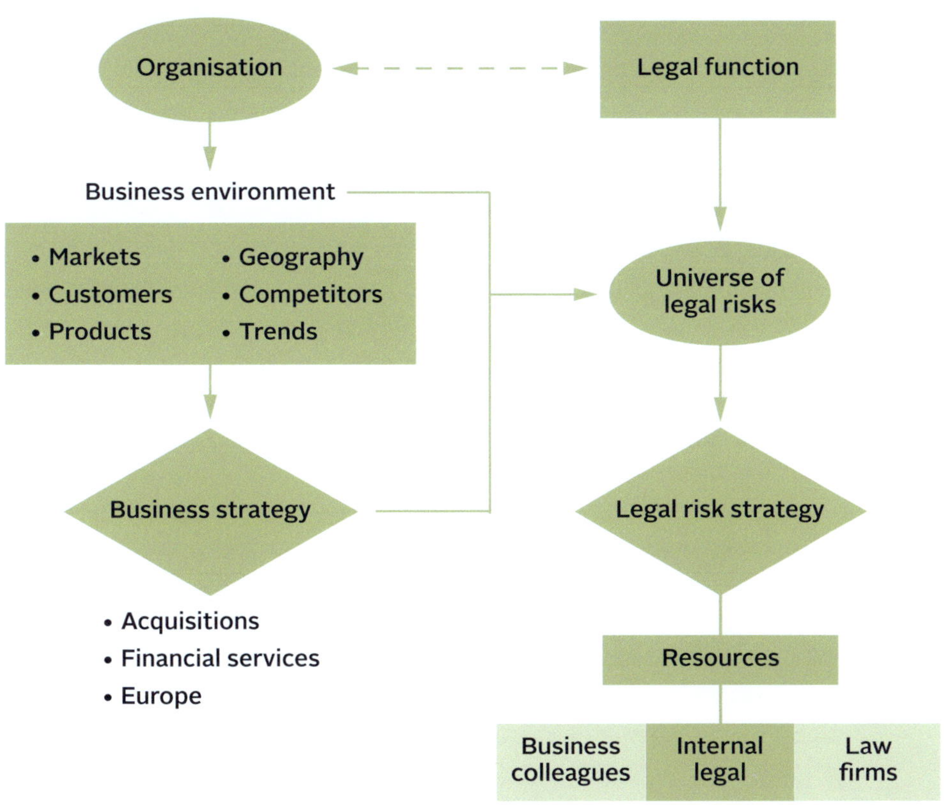

(a) What is your role and purpose?

The starting point is to define the role and purpose of the GC (and the legal function). There are two immediate points here. First, it is important to get the authority that this truly is your purpose as GC and head of legal. If there is an expectation that you will simply keep your head down and deal with everyday legal matters, then you may need to either challenge that or not waste time and energy on pursuing the bigger task.

Second, while the concept of opportunity may be obvious to you, it may not be obvious to others. There may be an assumption that the role of legal is simply to keep the business out of trouble. Most effective GCs that we know make a point of emphasising that they are always on the lookout for ways in which legal can actively contribute to the success of the business. That way, legal can avoid being labelled as 'the business prevention department' – the people who usually say 'no'.

(b) What universe of legal risks and opportunities needs to be covered by the strategy?

To answer this question, you need to consider your organisation/business from two perspectives:

"Most effective GCs that we know make a point of emphasising that they are always on the lookout for ways in which legal can actively contribute to the success of the business."

- the business environment in which it operates – markets, geography, products/services, competitors, trends (the sort of factors that a traditional SWOT analysis might identify); and
- the particular strategy that your business is pursuing – which is likely to be different from other businesses in the same sector and commercial environment. Is it expanding or retracting, moving into new markets or introducing new products and services?

This will provide the information and intelligence to answer the next question...

(c) What legal risks and opportunities impact on your organisation?
These might include protection of intellectual property, regulatory changes, breach of contract by suppliers, discrimination and employment claims, and failure to meet loan obligations. This will form the crux of your legal risk strategy. A little later, we suggest four potential core strategies which will be appropriate for most businesses.

(d) How will implementation of the legal risk strategy be resourced?
There are three options here:

- internal legal team;
- internal business colleagues; and
- external lawyers.

The balance will reflect the internal culture of the organisation. What role is the legal function – and in particular, the in-house legal team – expected to play? The answer to this question will also be influenced by what makes most economic sense.

For example, when one of us was based in the Europe, Middle East and Africa legal team of a major multinational, the small UK-based legal team was expected to be close (strategically and physically) to the senior management of the business. The internal team focused on commercial, regulatory and IP issues. Major 'bet-the-farm' transactions were handled by a magic circle firm and routine debt collection by two highly automated, process-driven national firms. The business also had a retainer arrangement with a medium-sized London firm, which was on call for litigation issues such as employment disputes. And then there were individual in-house lawyers in key capital cities and a network of trusted law firms around the region. At the same time, colleagues in departments such as marketing and security were aware of the legal issues that could arise in their areas of responsibility.

2.2 Generic strategies for in-house legal teams

There are potentially four core purposes for an in-house legal department, as outlined below. Which one (or possibly two) of these might apply to your team? We say one (or possibly two), because a legal department trying to do all four would be attempting the impossible and would lack focus.

(a) Cost advantage

- To get legal work done at minimum cost to the organisation – in terms of both:
  - work done internally (ie, at lower rates than would be charged by external law firms); and
  - the choice and control of external lawyers for work that does need to go outside.

(b) Governance

- To focus on compliance with regulatory issues that govern how the business can operate, which will involve looking outside at forthcoming changes in regulations and inside at standards of business behaviour (this will be particularly relevant in sectors such as financial services and pharmaceuticals); and
- To manage the quality and performance (not just cost) of external law firms.

(c) Competitive advantage

- To contribute to the business performance of the organisation – for example, in terms of new product development and IP development and protection; and
- To use the law to help the organisation gain an advantage over business rivals.

(d) Speed

- To operate on the front line alongside business colleagues to enable the business to make legal/business decisions in real time – for example, in financial services trading rooms. This may require legal systems rather than people to be alongside the business people.

The elevator test

A carefully thought-through and articulated strategy for legal can guide decision making about work allocation, recruitment, career development, relationships with other parts of the business and discussions with the board.

A simple and striking example of the benefit of a legal strategy is what we call the elevator test. Imagine that you are standing waiting for the lift on the ground floor, when the CEO walks up and stands

"A carefully thought-through and articulated strategy for legal can guide decision making about work allocation, recruitment, career development, relationships with other parts of the business and discussions with the board."

alongside you. They glance at you and ask the question, "So remind me: why is it that we have all you lawyers up on the fourth floor?" A reply of "Well, we're all very busy doing important work" probably won't cut it.

But "We're making sure that we can open for business tomorrow and that you and the directors don't go to jail" (ie, governance) would probably make an impact. As would "We help keep the business one step ahead of Competitor X" (ie, competitive advantage); or "We make sure that the maximum number of deals gets done as fast as possible" (ie, speed); or "We save money for the business by getting essential legal work done at minimum cost" (ie, cost).

Developing and sharing a response to the elevator test is a key component of having an effective legal strategy for the business.

V. Managing the legal team

In this chapter, we look at how the legal department needs to be managed as a 'business unit' in its own right and how the legal team interacts with other parts of the business.

(A word of warning here: we are extremely wary of making simple comparisons in order to determine the 'right' size of an in-house legal department or overall spend on legal. Two different organisations may each have a turnover of £500 million, but it may make complete sense for Company A to have six in-house lawyers and Company B to have 50; and for Company A to have a total legal spend of twice Company B. Any form of comparison is meaningful only if you have two businesses in the same sector facing a similar range of legal risks and with broadly similar business strategies.)

1. Finance

1.1 Budget

What is the budget for legal? This will need to cover the in-house team and external lawyers, and investment in people in the business who have a quasi-legal role. You may be building this from scratch. More likely, you will be inheriting a previous budget or a process for arriving at a legal budget. You will have an array of questions to consider:

- Does the budget cover all legal spending?
- Does it enable all of the key legal risks to be addressed?
- Could some tasks that are lawyer intensive be automated?
- Are external lawyers selected and managed on a rigorous basis?

1.2 Cost

Who pays for legal? Is the legal budget a central overhead or are the users of legal services (whether in-house or external lawyers) meant to pay? The latter approach has advantages and disadvantages. It dissuades other parts of the business from over-using legal services where the legal team is seen as a free resource; but then, you do want the business to consult the legal team where appropriate and not to be put off by concerns that their own budget will take a hit.

1.3 Time recording

This would seem to be most relevant if the in-house team is charging other parts of the organisation for its services. But just as in law firms, where there has been a move away from hourly charging rates towards fixed or capped fees, it is important to remember that the purpose of recording time spent is for internal efficiency, not charging. How many hours does it take to carry out a specific real estate transaction or negotiate a reoccurring contract? Does this vary by individual in-house lawyer? What explains variations – for example, the experience of the lawyer or the knowledge/helpfulness of the person in the business who is the client?

We would argue that full-time, across-the-board time recording is probably not appropriate; but a more selective approach might be. So, for a limited period of a couple of months, it could be worth tracking how everyone is spending their time or checking the time spent on a particular type of work.

2. Marketing/business development

It is obvious that in a law firm, marketing and business development are crucial. But what about in a legal department? It may be different, but it is still important. And just as in a law firm, business development is not just about getting more business, in the sense that any new business must be good for the organisation; it's about attracting the right type of work.

So, in your organisation, do the business units and key people in them know what the legal team can do for them? Do they appreciate when it's appropriate – and sometimes imperative – to consult legal? What legal education do they need so that they do not always need to check with legal? Do they know the best way to contact legal? Are there circumstances in which they can and should go straight to outside lawyers? (One of us recalls a decidedly heated and emotional

"We would argue that full-time, across-the-board time recording is probably not appropriate; but a more selective approach might be."

exchange on this last point at a conference of in-house lawyers. Some thought that in carefully controlled circumstances, it would be fine for business people to consult an outside law firm without going through the in-house legal team; others thought the very idea sacrilegious!)

Addressing these (and other) questions will require thought and planning within the legal team, and consultation with the relevant business units.

Taking a textbook approach to marketing/business development, an in-house legal team could look at the six 'Ps' of the marketing mix:

- **Product/service:** What are the services that you offer (and don't offer) – for example, yes for employment advice, but no for real estate (which goes to an outside firm)?
- **Place:** Where are the legal services available? In the virtual world, everyone and everything can be available everywhere. But there may be choices as to whether the legal team is located at head office or whether people are dispersed across the business – for example, having an employment lawyer on site at a large manufacturing plant in Bristol or IP lawyers in the Frankfurt office.
- **Price:** Do you charge and, if so, what do you charge? As

mentioned above, it's possible that a business may want its units to pay for legal services – or at least know what amount of the legal budget they are taking up by their use of legal resources.

- **People:** Do you have the people with the right legal, business and personal skills, so that the business will want to communicate and work with them?
- **Process:** How are legal services delivered? (We will look at this in more detail in section 4). In marketing terms, is it easy (rather than off-putting) to ask for advice and receive help from the legal team?
- **Promotion:** How can you persuasively communicate how legal can assist the business? A promotional campaign across the organisation could involve face-to-face meetings, training, online FAQs and other communications techniques that explain the benefits of the legal team and how best to work with it.

3. HR

An important aspect of the role of the GC is to build and develop their team of lawyers and (if relevant) support staff. Many will have had experience of this as a partner or head of department in a law firm. One key difference here is that their new organisation will be accustomed to recruiting and developing the mainstream

"How can you persuasively communicate how legal can assist the business? A promotional campaign across the organisation could involve face-to-face meetings, training, online FAQs and other communications techniques that explain the benefits of the legal team."

professionals and workers in the business – whether engineers, bankers, IT experts, retail managers and staff or scientists. This could be quite a mind shift for a lawyer who is used to lawyers being the mainstream professionals – they will now learn what it feels like to be in a business development or HR role in a law firm!

In our view, the role of the GC as a coach and/or mentor is so important that, although it falls naturally under this section, we have devoted an entire chapter to the topic later in this Special Report.

In the meantime, we would make one observation here, based on conversations with GCs over the years: a few sometimes report, with a great sense of pride, that they have increased their in-house legal team from, say, 12 to 16 people over the course of the last year. But this makes us wonder why this is a good thing in itself. It's possible that it may be, if there are compelling strategic (as opposed to egocentric) reasons why that was necessary. But otherwise, why is it of benefit to the business to increase the size and cost of a support function? Again, think back to being a partner in a law firm and how you might react to the head of HR giving you similar news.

Let's take a look at some of the key HR activities that a GC is involved in.

3.1 Recruiting and inducting

Of course, help may well be on hand here from the organisation's own HR function. This will be important to ensure that lawyers joining the organisation share (or can fit in with, or maybe even disrupt) the style, culture and values of the mainstream people already there. For example, there may be a greater use of psychometrics in recruitment than would be usual in a law firm.

A standard way to approach recruitment is to think of the job description and then the person specification:

- **Job description:** What is the job/role and what set of tasks needs to be performed? If this is a new role, the job description may need to be developed from scratch. If it is to replace someone who is leaving, this may be easier. But beware making the assumption that the job will be the same, and that the sort of person you need will be the same too. This could be a chance to extend the role and provide a service that the team was not previously offering. Or it may be helpful to carve out part of the old role and give it to someone more junior as part of their career development.
- **Person specification:** What range of skills, qualifications, experience and attitudes does the new person need to have –

or have the potential to develop? Do they need to fit in with the existing team? Or can they add diversity, in terms of background or experience, to the existing team?

There may be (or you may want to develop) a competency framework that details what is expected of someone who does a particular job at a particular level of seniority.

When it comes to the recruitment process, again, the organisation may have its standard procedures. These may well range further than the standard interview format. You may want to consider the following options:

- a trial task;
- a presentation;
- an informal 'meet the team' session;
- a more strictly competency-based interview (ie, where the focus is on actual experience rather than general assertions or attitudes); and
- a deliberately more diverse interview panel.

It may also be useful to consider whether there is a bias towards a particular style within your team (eg, studious introverts or lively extroverts) and you want more of a balance. Will your recruitment process work for different types of people?

3.2 Learning and development

(a) Learning

The GC plays a vital role in helping their team to develop existing skills and learn new skills, and to build their experience in a thoughtful and planned way, rather than relying on happenstance.

A key stage – which we certainly appreciated in our journey from lawyers to management consultants and business coaches – is learning about how people learn. We have encountered many professionals for whom this was also a real 'lightbulb' moment. People learn in different ways. We are all likely to have a preference – and then, quite likely, to assume that our preferred style of learning is the obvious and best way for everyone else to learn; and perhaps to be mildly (or not so mildly) annoyed if other people approach learning in a different way.

Researchers and authors Honey and Mumford[8] have developed one of the best-known models of learning. It identifies four stages in the learning process and then links them to four preferred styles of learning. The four stages are:

- having an experience;
- reviewing an experience;
- concluding from the experience; and
- planning the next steps.

Let's take a concrete example to illustrate. Alex, a young in-house lawyer, is going to run a meeting with a business colleague and an external lawyer. It's the first time he has done this – or maybe the first time he has attended such an important meeting of this type.

During the meeting, there is a radical departure from the agenda that Alex was hoping to follow. The external lawyer does most of the talking, when Alex wanted his business colleague to be the major contributor; and the meeting overruns, so Alex has to finish it before some important issues are discussed. This is 'having an experience'.

Later that day, and over the next few days, Alex 'reviews the experience'. This could be quietly on his own, almost subconsciously; or in a more explicit way, in a conversation with the GC or someone else. He becomes more aware of what happened during the meeting by reviewing it mentally or by describing it out loud.

"The GC plays a vital role in helping their team to develop existing skills and learn new skills, and to build their experience in a thoughtful and planned way, rather than relying on happenstance."

Then Alex starts to think about lessons learned from the meeting – about the dos and don'ts for next time. This is 'concluding from the experience'. Maybe he asks someone for advice or consults a blog or TED talk on running meetings, thinking about how to do it better next time.

Finally, when another such meeting comes up, Alex plans and prepares for it in a different way: being clearer about the agenda; saying upfront what he wants from the different people at the meeting; stressing the time constraints and the need to cover all the ground. This is 'planning the next steps': putting into practice what was learned from the other stages of the process. And then we come full circle: Alex has another meeting and has an experience once again.

The associated styles of learning are as follows:

- Activist: People who like to learn by just having a go – doing something and then doing it again, getting stuck in.
- Reflector: People who prefer to stand back and review and reflect on what they have done and the consequences, working things out carefully.

"One way to ensure that the development of your team does not get neglected is to accept accountability for it: it becomes part of your job description and is subject to review by whoever you report to and appraises your performance."

- Pragmatist: People who prefer to learn by solving problems, trying out ideas, coming up with and implementing practical solutions.
- Theorists: People who want to find out, understand and put into action the logical way, the 'right' way, of doing something – for example, by reading a book or going on a course.

You can probably see how a theorist could get frustrated with what to them might appear to be the 'bull in a china shop' approach of the activist; while the activist might want the theorist to just get on and run another meeting, rather than going off on a time-consuming course on running meetings. And so on.

We all adapt and learn in different ways, and sometimes circumstances mean that we have to learn in a certain way. If you think about a driving test – yes, there's a theory test, but it's probably a good thing for everyone that it also involves a practical test!

The takeaway for GCs – and for all of us – is to think carefully about the different ways in which people can be helped to learn effectively and cover the full range, from encouraging people to try things out to formal and informal feedback, coaching and mentoring, and more formal development programmes.

(b) Development

As you assess your department as a whole and the individuals in your team, you will be asking yourself, "What do we need to get better at and be able to do that we don't currently do?" This might involve adding an area of legal expertise or understanding a part of the business better, or building a closer relationship with the board. Some of these will be issues that are important, but not urgent, and can thus easily be put off due to the day-to-day demands of business clients.

One way to ensure that the development of your team does not get neglected is to accept accountability for it: it becomes part of your job description and is subject to review by whoever you report to and appraises your performance. Of course, one group of people who will definitely know whether you are focusing on development will be the members of your in-house team themselves; so seek out their feedback and ideas.

In our experience, one way to combine organisational effectiveness with the opportunity for development is through a form of matrix management within your team. This probably works best for small and medium-sized teams of, say, four to 10 lawyers. Each lawyer can be allocated three or four areas of responsibility, such as:

- a legal specialism;
- a geographic area;
- a business unit; and
- an internal role.

So, for example, one lawyer could look after commercial contracts/the west of England/sales and marketing/knowledge management for the in-house team; and another intellectual property/South America/the R&D department/in-house social activities. By allocating team members a responsibility that might be beyond their current experience (or comfort zone), this affords the opportunity for development; as does switching around responsibilities after a period of, say, two years, so that people gain greater experience. At least to start with, you will probably want volunteers rather than conscripts for these matrix responsibilities.

(c) Rewards

How your team is rewarded will almost certainly be dictated by wider organisational policies. But you will probably want to have a say and introduce some flexibility that takes into account the particular role of the in-house lawyer. The basic salary and benefits will need to be compatible with other professionals and executives within the organisation, and capable of attracting good lawyers from private practice.

But what else can you do? More than ever post-COVID-19, flexible and agile working will be on the agenda. This may have become part of the 'new normal'. Some people will have loved not coming into the office; preferred Zoom to face-to-face meetings; enjoyed more time with family or for exercise. As one of our colleagues remarked, the pandemic is a great time to be an introvert, with the style and efficiency of quieter workers being very much appreciated in the absence of the louder, outgoing types around the office.

Much has been and will be written about the longer-term effects of the pandemic – inevitably much of it speculative, but still thought provoking. There may be a virtuous triple whammy of organisations saving money on office space, people having a better work/life balance and reduced commuting and pollution. People may have got used to and really value a more flexible schedule that allows them, for example, to get to choir practice at 7:00pm every Thursday or to start work at 7:00am and take the dog out for a walk as a long mid-morning break. The point is that this flexibility may be an easier reward to give now than it was in 2019.

4. Operations

The idea of getting legal work done effectively and efficiently is important, and yet so obvious that in the past it has been overlooked.

"The idea of getting legal work done effectively and efficiently is important, and yet so obvious that in the past it has been overlooked."

The whole area of operations management – which is vital to most businesses that either manufacture products (whether cars, mobile phones or wind turbines) or deliver services (whether healthcare, insurance or education) – is now mainstream in legal services too. The idea that (in a private practice setting) two partners in the same firm sitting yards apart would approach a recurring transaction such as an M&A deal in entirely different ways because "That's how I prefer to do it" is fading fast, if not completely gone, in most well-managed firms.

Even more so in-house, the emphasis is now on developing and monitoring systems and processes that can get work done faster, cheaper and better.

As GC, you will want to review not only what work is kept in-house, but also how it is processed. What can be automated using current technology or emerging AI? How can knowledge management tools facilitate a quicker, more consistent turnaround of documents? Can junior lawyers be enabled to do work currently done by senior lawyers? What opportunities exist for your team and external lawyers to work together seamlessly?

This is a specialist area and outside the scope of this brief Special Report to cover fully. Expert advice is available and can be very helpful.

5. Reflections on the legal team

In the course of your work as an in-house lawyer, you will deal with many different people, teams and departments. These will extend from the board downwards. It is always useful to ask for feedback from the people you work with, to see how effective they consider you and the legal team to be. We spoke to Martin Spencer of See Level Consulting, a psychologist and former HR director, about his dealings with in-house lawyers:

> *I can't remember any discussions with a GC about points of law and I would generally go externally for this. The value of the in-house team is in recommending external lawyers and acting as an interpreter, so the emphasis is on the 'general' – although the 'counsel' is still important. The great benefit of the GC is that they can contextualise an issue and advise accordingly because they understand the organisation, its culture and people. It has to be a confidential and trusted partnership – I have needed to be able to fully trust the in-house legal team and to bounce ideas off them. It is a collaboration. Effective GCs understand my risk appetite or get to understand it and take this into consideration in advising me. Any frustrations? Only when the GC sits on the fence or is unduly pedantic – I need an effective solution to my issue.*

VI. Building your department

1. The importance of teams

The late David Nadler, a renowned corporate governance expert, once wrote this about boards: "The high performance board, like the high performance team, is competent, co-ordinated, collegial, and focused on an unambiguous goal. Such entities do not simply evolve; they must be constructed to an exacting blueprint."[9]

His reference to teams is important: if you are going to succeed in your role as a GC, you are going to need to build your team. You may, of course, be a team of one or have gone in as the first in-house lawyer. While you will still have to manage yourself, there may come a time when you need to recruit or to take on other roles, so this section also applies to you too. But back to Nadler: while he talked about many of the components that high-performance teams require, the most important statement is that effective teams must be built – they don't just appear by luck. So how do you build a high-performing team?

2. Be clear on the strategy

Strategy is covered elsewhere in this book. Suffice to say here that you need to have a clear idea of where you are going that accords with the company's own strategy; otherwise, you are likely to achieve little. As Lewis Carroll wrote: "If you don't know where you want to go, then it doesn't matter which path you take."[10] This is not a recipe for success;

so have a clear but succinct plan of what you want your department to achieve and cover, and the timeframe for doing so. It needs to be succinct, because it must be clearly understood by the business – and more importantly, you! Don't make it too complex – it could be as simple as a 12-month plan, including:

- the types of work to be covered;
- the legal documents to be dealt with in-house and those to be outsourced;
- how different business areas will be supported;
- the support expected from the business;
- the shape of the external legal panel; and
- what the legal team is expected to look like in a year's time.

You also need to focus on the fact that the strategy is bound to have to change. If we had said back in 2019 that it was likely that your team would all be working from home in 2020 and would only visit the office a couple of times that year, you would have quickly disbelieved us (and if we had been providing consulting services, quickly sacked us!). Circumstances can change very quickly, so you have to be able to adapt to that change at a similar pace. This was brought home to us by Colonel Bob Stewart,[11] who said that strategy on the battlefield often has to be completely changed – he used the example of a simple strategy for a tank commander being rewritten every time the tank was bombed. Hopefully, you will never be in this situation; but Stewart's straightforward assessment of strategic direction (he called it 'mission analysis') is one worth keeping close to heart.

3. Devise a plan

Tip: Have a clear but straightforward and succinct strategy for your team, and keep it under review.

3.1 Understand the business

The next key stage in managing your team is to ensure that you and they understand the business. In-house lawyers do change sectors from time to time (although this is less frequent these days), and if this is the case it can take time to get up to speed with a new sector – particularly if it is a regulated one. But sooner or later, you must understand what your business does and how it works. As one of us once wrote:

> *Lawyers need to see themselves as business people first, who happen to have a legal background. To do so, they really need to understand the business. This is more difficult than it sounds. It is not simply about knowing the organisation's products and how they work – though these are both important – but understanding the*

culture, the people, the internal workings and the external (macro) market.[12]

We will come on to culture, but understanding how your particular organisation works is crucial. Who are the power brokers? How can you best influence how to get things done? What are the best ways of getting things done? Equally, what are the things that you shouldn't do?

3.2 Set the mandate

The trouble with being an in-house lawyer – particularly if you are the first lawyer in the business – is that the mandate can quickly get out of control. You can end up being the go-to person for everything – and this is often exacerbated if you are also the company secretary. Try as you might, this is a battle that you won't win! You can't do everything, especially if your resources are limited; and while you may want to make a good impression if you are new, your reputation will quickly be tarnished if you get swamped. This applies irrespective of whether the legal department has many lawyers or just one. So be clear on what your role covers – and more importantly, what it does not! One of the first things you might want to do with your CEO is to agree the mandate – both of your role as GC and of the department as a whole.

"Understanding how your particular organisation works is crucial. Who are the power brokers? How can you best influence how to get things done? What are the best ways of getting things done? Equally, what are the things that you shouldn't do?"

The document should be simple and succinct, setting out the main areas that you and your team will cover; that way, it can be sent to other employees, to outline which things they can bother you with – and which they can't! (Don't make it a long document: in these times of bite-sized information, people won't read it and the purpose will be defeated.) You will still get asked from time to time to do things that aren't within your remit; but if you have an agreed mandate with the backing of your CEO, you can easily say no (in a nice way, of course – one of us once acted as a mentor to a fantastically clever GC who knew the law backwards, but used to bark "No!" at the business whenever he was asked to do something outside his area of responsibility. There are ways to say no that will win you friends rather than creating enemies!).

In setting the mandate, GCs should take care to avoid being tempted into scope creep. This is something that is perhaps peculiar to lawyers – we think that we can do everything, that everyone else's job is easy and that we can take it on if we need to and/or want to. But this is an arrogance which is misplaced. One of us recalls listening to a GC whom he admired enormously. The GC was complaining about the CEO's lukewarm reception of his attempts to share strategic input at executive team meetings: "I want my CEO to know I have views on

"It is better to be a very effective GC who doesn't sit on the exco than an ineffective one who does. Good executive teams and CEOs normally know when to consult the GC."

strategy – it is an area where I (as a lawyer) clearly have expertise and he should be listening to me!" Now, while accepting that as a member of the exco, you may have the opportunity to contribute to the debate on the wider running of the business, you need to remember why you are sitting there: because of your legal expertise. Few CEOs worth their salt will start asking the marketing director for legal advice; and neither should you assume that you are there to run the strategic agenda for the organisation. Unless you have specific training in the area of strategy or HR or marketing, you should leave it to those who do. So while you will inevitably get involved in other areas of the business, ensure that you are clear about your mandate. Running the legal team successfully is no mean feat in itself – trying to take on the world is best avoided!

This also leads us to the debate as to whether the GC should sit on the exco. We must confess that we used to be clearly in the pro camp: "The GC is so important that they just have to be part of the exco – how could the company operate successfully if they were not?" Sitting on the exco does give you access to how the business is being run and what is going on (just as access to the board does, as we discuss later). However, it is not essential. One of us remembers a very renowned GC saying that things always started going wrong if the GC wasn't on the exco, so he always insisted on being a member. A few years later, the company that he worked for became mired in a major scandal – his presence on the exco had made no difference, it would appear! The most important thing is to focus on your role as GC. If being an exco member will distract from that, then ask yourself whether it is key. However important the GC role may be, it will never hold the same importance as, for example, that of CFO. It is better to be a very effective GC who doesn't sit on the exco than an ineffective one who does. Good executive teams and CEOs normally know when to consult the GC.

Tip: Agree the mandate – both of your role as GC and of the department as a whole – with the CEO and, if necessary, the board. Again, make it succinct and clear.

3.3 Create a service level agreement

One simple way to set expectations is to draw up a simple service level agreement (SLA) between you and the business. This will help you to review the legal team and what is expected from it by the business.

One of us, as a consultant, undertook a review of a European legal team that appeared to have a disconnect from the business. While the legal team knew there were issues, it did not realise the extent of them. By having a consultant asking both the business people and the lawyers what they expected from each other and how they could best

"To some extent, the culture of the legal team will mirror that of the organisation it serves as a whole. But this is not to forget that the legal team needs to retain its independence to be a successful adviser to the business."

work together, it became possible to address some of the issues and get the lawyers working more effectively with the business (previously, the department was seen as an external firm of lawyers sitting within a major company). As part of this, a straightforward SLA was created, outlining the major things that each party wanted and expected from the other. The key here is to keep it simple. Don't be tempted to recreate a complex legal agreement – after all, you are working for the same side (or you should be!). And you want something that will be read, understood and complied with both by the business and by the legal department. So you might want to include matters such as the following:

- the expectations of the legal department and the business in dealing with matters. For example, if you are going to review a contract on behalf of the business, you might expect that they will have read it first and have a list of points they want to raise (you would be surprised how many times a contract is just sent to the legal department 'for review' without the business having ever looked at it!). Equally, you might want to make it clear that the commercial terms are a matter for the business and they should be confident about them. This leads to a more important point: the SLA should be 'owned' by the business and not by the legal department. If you are just being used as a means of validation – "The legal department said it was okay" is a common statement when a problem subsequently arises with the contract – then something is wrong;

- the types of briefings that the legal team needs to work with a matter;
- the types of matters that the legal team will deal with and the types it won't (should you be spending time reviewing the watercooler agreement when it is a standard, unamendable contract?), and the types of work that will be outsourced;
- a clear indication of whether the business can instruct external lawyers directly and, if so, who can be used for particular types of work and how the legal team should be kept informed on matters (not least the costs!);
- the approximate timescales to deal with a matter (where there is a deadline, make sure that it is specified and workable);
- a commitment by both sides to getting the matter achieved on time;
- the main points of contact for particular matters;
- the areas of expertise and specialism in the legal team;
- how to raise matters if things go wrong; and
- how often the relationship between the business and the legal team will be reviewed and who will do this.

Much of what you include within the SLA will accord with your strategy, as outlined above.

Tip: Create a service level agreement to set expectations in accordance with your strategy.

3.4 Creating the culture for the team

To some extent, the culture of the legal team will mirror that of the organisation it serves as a whole. But this is not to forget that the legal team needs to retain its independence to be a successful adviser to the business. In a report entitled *Corporate Culture and the Role of Boards* published by the Financial Reporting Council, Sir Win Bischoff stated:

> *A healthy culture both protects and generates value. It is therefore important to have a continuous focus on culture, rather than wait for a crisis. Poor behaviour can be exacerbated when companies come under pressure. A strong culture will endure in times of stress and mitigate the impact. This is essential in dealing effectively with risk and maintaining resilient performance.*[13]

Anecdotal evidence suggests that most senior executives who fail in their role do so not on the grounds of competence (or incompetence) or knowledge, but rather due to lack of cultural fit. While skills will be important when creating, designing or redesigning your team, cultural fit will be even more so. You may have all the skills covered for a really effective department, but if the members don't fit the culture of the business, it will be dysfunctional. This is important because recruiters rarely seem to focus on this and just hone in on skills or experience, rather than seeing the wider picture. One of us was once interviewed for a senior role at a household-name company. The head-hunter – very skilled in his craft – told him that he had all the skills and competencies needed and could be put forward for the role if he wanted, but that he would never fit the culture. While he was slightly stung at the time, this turned out to be wise counsel. The same is true of you as the GC when you put your team together – you need people who will fit the culture of the team and the organisation. What values do they have? How do they want to work together? Will they be a team or a group of individuals? Are they aligned to the company's values, purpose and products? If, for example, the company operates in the gambling or tobacco sector, will they feel comfortable with that? Setting the culture for your team is one of the first things that you should do in your role. Of course, if your team already exists, that may mean making some difficult decisions and changes. If the team is a start-up, you will have a freer hand.

Allied to creating the right culture is ensuring the wellbeing of your team. Wellbeing has been very much in focus in recent years and is likely to remain so given the recent move to working from home during the COVID-19 crisis. Part of this can be achieved through good coaching and mentoring (more on which later). However, ensuring the health and wellbeing of your team members is one of your prime duties, as well as being enshrined in law. As my colleague Paul Gilbert puts it:

> *I suspect we are victims of what has happened to very many people, not just lawyers, in all walks of life. We are all swept along by the need to be more efficient, to cut costs and to do more with less. We have all assumed technology (especially email) has helped us do our jobs better, when in reality it has just made us more available for longer and blurred boundaries between work and home. In-house lawyers, however, I think are dealing with even more than this. This is not special pleading, but in-house lawyers… lack infrastructure to support their roles, are without significant peer support and soak up the pressure heaped on them by work colleagues who have their own stresses to manage. It can be a lonely and attritional environment.*[14]

So remember: culture first, skills second. Speaking of which…

3.5 Recruiting for your team and succession planning

If you have a close relationship with the business – you have developed your strategy and produced an SLA – then you should have a good idea of what skills your team is going to need. However, unless you are in one of the very largest legal departments, remember that you won't be able to cover every skill you need. Lawyers, like other managers, often treat recruitment as a secondary matter to be dealt with only when the (immediate) need arises. That is a mistake. You should plan for succession and review your plan regularly to meet the needs of the business and respond to changes within your team. You never know when you might lose a team member unexpectedly, so you have to keep on top of this. Building good relationships with respected head-hunters is key, as you need to know who you can trust. Below, Brian Littleton, head of in-house legal recruitment (London) for Chadwick Nott, gives some tips on recruitment strategy for the GC.

Tips: recruitment strategy

- Be aware that every role probably has a shelf life and that each team member will need a new challenge at some stage. In a small team with limited opportunities, it is expected that candidates will need to move after a certain period of time – typically three to five years.
- Always have a succession plan in place, unless the GC has recently been appointed or promoted and is evaluating the team and their skillsets.
- Constantly appraise changing market dynamics that distort existing business models and build a team with that mindset. The IT and fast-moving consumer goods sectors are most vulnerable to rapidly changing market dynamics from disruptors and technology changes.
- Be able to pivot the direction of the team when a major change occurs in the market. On that point, most strategy consultants from the top three consultancies undertake work to react to changing market dynamics – COVID-19, Brexit and base rates of 0.1% being prime examples. Often, only 10% of strategy is focused on blue-sky thinking for possible future events.
- Adopt a fluid approach that allows new ideas to be evaluated at regular intervals – say, every three to six months – even if everything is running smoothly.
- Evaluate resourcing requirements every three to six months as a matter of course at management/board meetings.
- Have a clear mandate for the team and its expected output, and communicate to the board the team's indirect and significant value-adding ability to the bottom line. Gaps in output and overuse of law firms may give rise to an extra hire or an interim hire to plug the gap or reduce costs. Day-rate hires often don't count as headcount.
- Have relationships with one or two head-hunters with market knowledge who can be called upon at short notice – especially on salary.

These are all good points. Something else to note is that you have to help manage the careers of your team, which may lead to some difficult decisions for both you and them. Not everyone can be GC, and if you are firmly ensconced in your role and liked by the business, you may decide that you are not going anywhere! This means that ambitious members of your team have a choice to make: either stay put or move on elsewhere if they aspire to a more senior role. Having honest and regular conversations about prospects will help both you and your team. If it does turn out that they need to move on, then setting expectations and helping your team members will assist you with succession planning and keep them as allies – you never know when you might need them in the future. Equally, where you have a large team made up of generalists and specialists, you may have to see how you can develop the careers of the latter. As one of us wrote elsewhere:

> *Law Departments, like many others, are becoming less hierarchical. This trend is likely to increase rather than diminish in the future. One of the common challenges for in-house lawyers in the past has been whether to be a specialist or generalist. It is an important decision because specialists are valued for their distinct legal expertise which has led to them being kept in their specialism rather than climb the ladder to more general management. However, the move towards flatter management structures means that in the future even generalist lawyers will find the climb to General Counsel more challenging, however good they are.*[15]

Seniority and pay often accompany a management role, which may mean leaving your specialism behind. Not all lawyers want to manage people – indeed, many do not – while others want to remain as specialists. You might need to think of innovative ways to reward these people or risk losing them. A major component of your role as an effective GC and manager is to help and develop the people in your team – to build their careers just as you build your team as a whole. Of course, this may mean that you lose people from time to time, but you will gain others and your team should be more effective as a result: good people will be more willing to join and remain in a department where the GC cares about them and helps them to develop their careers. You should regularly review with your team – both on an individual basis and as a group – what their aspirations are, what work they want to do, what work they should be doing and equally what work they should not be doing. One of the best people we have seen doing this in practice was the CEO of a large set of barristers' chambers, who built the careers of many future QCs and judges by listening carefully to what members' aspirations were and ensuring that they did the right type of work. That often meant turning away work in order to develop their practice. As one QC told us: "If I hadn't listened to the CEO and let him manage my career, I would never have become a silk – let alone undertaken some of the major cases I did in the second half of my career."

So ensure that you manage your team. To assist in doing so, you might like to sit the whole team down once or twice a year and ask some searching questions, such as the following:

- How do we best work with each other?
- How do we best work with the business?
- What do we expect from each other?
- How can we best help each other?
- What behaviours are acceptable?
- And what are not?
- What have we achieved this year so far?
- What have been the good points?
- And the not so good ones?

4. And finally ...

Remember that you have the resources of many other professionals within the business to draw upon if you need help and advice on running the legal team. Lawyers are often critical of HR departments,

"A major component of your role as an effective GC and manager is to help and develop the people in your team – to build their careers just as you build your team as a whole."

but a good HR director or manager can help you to build and develop your team and provide support when issues arise. You should also:

- have regular one-to-ones with department heads where you provide material support. One of us used to have quarterly one-to-ones in his role as a GC – this was a good opportunity to discuss major matters that were affecting particular departments, as well as a way to get to know department heads; and
- if you report to the CEO, keep them regularly informed of what is going on and operate on a 'no surprises' basis. It sounds obvious, but this is often neglected and can end up tarnishing the relationship. From personal experience, we can testify that hiding from the CEO because things are not going well is not a course of action to be recommended! Having a regular dialogue will save both time and headaches.

VII. Coaching and mentoring

1. Coaching

Coaching can be a useful tool both for you in your role as a GC and for members of your team. While this is generally done on an individual basis, team coaching is now in vogue and is something that you might also consider for your department as a whole. Below we explain what coaching is, when it is appropriate and the value that can be gained from coaching. Much of what is written below is from *The Sherwood Coaching Handbook*, which you can find at www.sherwoodpsfconsulting.com.

1.1 What is coaching and what is its purpose?

To answer the second question first – effective coaching enables people to maximise their potential and perform to the very best of their ability. Coaching is designed to be of benefit to the individual and to the organisation in which they work. In fact, one of the building blocks to a successful coaching relationship (between the individual, the coach and the organisation) is an agreed vision of what all parties want to achieve.

A typical coaching session involves a one-to-one discussion over a period of one to two hours. It can be preceded by a telephone call or a virtual conversation to establish the purpose of the session and/or the key points to be addressed, and to see whether there is any preparatory work that either the coach or individual should do. Afterwards, there may be a follow-up telephone call to review progress.

If a face-to-face meeting is impractical, a coaching session can take the form of a telephone/virtual conversation once the coach and individual have established a good working relationship.

Depending on the reason for engaging in coaching, there will usually be a series of meetings or, more unusually, a single, one-off session as appropriate.

The role of the coach is to work with the individual to:

- increase their professional self-awareness in terms of their work, their role, how they approach it and their underlying motivation;
- identify what is going well and what is not, understand the causes and determine what could help them to perform at a higher level;
- take responsibility for making any appropriate changes that will enable them to perform at that higher level – what they need to stop, start or carry on doing, or do differently; and
- sustain and/or improve personal and business performance.

"External coaches may have particular sector or role experience that provides credibility and can be a source of useful insights."

The style of the coach will generally be 'non-directive'. The coach is not there as a trainer or expert adviser telling the individual what to do. Instead, in a coaching session, the coach will spend a lot of time asking questions that help (and even force) the individual to think about their work and working relationships in a deeper way than they have done, or had the opportunity to do, in the past.

In this context, a coach needs to be good at:

- prompting the appropriate self-reflection on the part of the individual – for instance, by asking the appropriate question at the optimal moment;
- listening in an attentive and open-minded way;
- encouraging and helping the individual to develop their own goals, ideas, options and plans; and
- challenging where necessary to test assumptions, clarify thinking and, if required, hold the individual to account for what they commit to doing.

The end point of a coaching session will usually be a practical plan for specific action to which the individual is committed: something concrete – not just a vague feeling of wellbeing.

It is helpful here to distinguish between coaching and mentoring. A mentor brings some sector and/or role-specific knowledge to the table – that is, in relation to the individual, they have 'been there, seen it, done it' too. Of course, coaching and mentoring can overlap – with powerful results. External coaches may have particular sector or role experience that provides credibility and can be a source of useful insights. Equally, however, there can be an advantage in having a coach who doesn't have knowledge of your profession or sector, as the temptation to 'interfere' and impose their own views can be a material disadvantage.

1.2 When can coaching be of value?

Examples include the following:

- when someone takes on (or aspires to) a new role and new challenges through promotion or a change in responsibilities, such as heading up a business group or function;
- when building and leading high-performance teams becomes a key element of an individual's job – in short, they need to be a coach to their team;
- when steering a business or organisation through significant change is the priority for someone in a leadership role;
- for new or existing teams that need to work well and achieve results together; or

- if creating a learning and coaching culture is required across an organisation.

1.3 When is coaching appropriate?

Examples include the following:

- when an established leader seeking to implement change and/or facing difficult decisions wants an independent and confidential sounding board;
- following (or preparing for) promotion, when someone wants to understand and meet new expectations – for example, becoming a partner or board member, or working in a new environment;
- when there is a need to get to grips with a new role following a lateral career move – for example, to chief executive, head of department or senior manager. This could involve support through the first 100 days (see Chapter III);
- when developing new skills, especially interpersonal skills, is a priority – for example, to run team meetings, hold important one-to-one conversations or appraisals, or manage conflict. Many otherwise confident and experienced professionals can struggle when strong emotions (their own or those of others) surface and have to be addressed;
- when a new team is created or an existing team is given a new task, and needs to explore how to work together most effectively;
- when a high-performing professional is interested in exploring motivation and discovering the next big challenge; or
- when an individual needs to prepare for a specific challenge – for example, putting together a business case, presenting to a new client, speaking at a conference or taking part in a selection day for promotion.

In each of these situations, coaching offers tailored support that can accelerate the individual's (or team's) learning, effectiveness and development. The focus is on helping people to raise and maintain their game.

An external coach who has some shared experience with the individual (eg, who has been a partner or senior manager in a law firm or similar business) may be able to combine the benefits of coaching and mentoring; but it is important to define the parameters of the coaching here if this is the case.

"Coaching offers tailored support that can accelerate the individual's (or team's) learning, effectiveness and development. The focus is on helping people to raise and maintain their game."

1.4 When is coaching (at least on its own) not appropriate?

Coaching is not appropriate when what the person really needs is:

- technical training;
- effective line management; or
- therapy or counselling (responsible business coaches should not stray into areas where they are not qualified to help – although they can act as a catalyst for a client who needs this to seek appropriate support elsewhere).

Finally, effective coaching is built on the assumption (which may need testing) that the individual is a volunteer, and has the physical and psychological energy to set and work towards challenging goals.

1.5 How to find the right coach

There are four options:

- outside coaching specialists;
- senior managers in leadership roles, such as CEOs and COOs, department heads or practice group leaders;
- other senior managers in the business from completely different areas of work from the relevant individual who are naturally good coaches and part of an internal coaching support network; and

- senior support professionals, such as the business development or HR directors.

The pros and cons of each option are explored below.

(a) Outside coaching specialists
These people will have the appropriate coaching skills: asking good questions, listening well and helping people to take responsibility. They will not bring assumptions, baggage or personal agendas into the relationship with the individual. They can be objective and see or raise issues that may not be apparent to people within the organisation.

The confidential nature of the coaching relationship enables trust to be established, which may not be possible where there is an expectation of internal reporting back. The individual may therefore be prepared to talk about issues (whether ambitions or perceived weaknesses) that they might withhold from someone within the organisation.

Outside coaches, however, may not understand the culture of the organisation or the realities of the working life of your people – or at least, that may be the perception of the individual. Having sector-specific knowledge can bridge this potential credibility gap, but is not essential. Lack of sector-specific knowledge can sometimes be a benefit, to help challenge norms of performance or expectations.

(b) Senior managers in leadership roles
These people may be obvious candidates to undertake a coaching role – they will know the person and the circumstances. But what they may lack are the skills, the inclination and, importantly, the time. Some senior managers will be able to adopt an effective coaching style and still be a demanding boss who, for example, carries out performance appraisals. Others will find it difficult to combine these approaches. In addition, exceptional sector-specific expertise can get in the way of an effective coaching relationship. The 'expert' may feel more comfortable addressing issues of technical competence, but this may be missing the point.

(c) Other senior managers
Some of the best coaches can be within the organisation, but not be technical experts in the same field as the person being coached. An interesting experiment was carried out in the sports world which revealed that under certain circumstances, ski coaches performed better than tennis coaches at coaching tennis! This was because the ski instructors were forced to focus more on listening to and understanding the person they were working with, rather than focusing on the correct technique. This is the so-called 'inner game',

in which the opponent in tennis or the barrier to top performance in golf is the voice inside our head saying what we must, should or ought to do, rather than the person on the other side of the net or the difficulty of the golf shot! A senior manager from another department who is not going to tell the individual how to do their job and is not going to carry out their next appraisal may get a better reception than the boss.

To assume this role, senior managers should have some natural aptitude and a willingness to learn more about coaching. It is then a matter of finding or creating opportunities for them to practise.

This approach can create a group of people with credibility who have a positive impact on the performance of others, and at the same time maybe break down unhealthy divisions between teams or departments. We usually find that developing coaching skills also makes people more effective in leading and managing their own people as part of their 'day job'.

(d) Business service professionals
Coaching by senior business services or support professionals (who are not formally trained coaches) can be very effective within their

"Developing coaching skills makes people more effective in leading and managing their own people as part of their 'day job'."

area of responsibility – for example, a business development director coaching on running pitches or a HR director coaching on how to facilitate better teamwork.

A qualified professional may prefer the opportunity of a one-to-one conversation rather than going on a traditional training programme, which may be seen as the 'remedial' option. Again, it will be a question of the business support person having the appropriate style, skills and time.

In fact, some organisations are now investing in coaching training for their senior business services professionals and recognising that coaching is a key part of their role.

1.6 How to get value from coaching

Given the confidential nature of the relationship between coach and individual, there can obviously be some issues for the budget holder as to how to ensure that the organisation gets value for money from this investment. In some coaching relationships – perhaps those involving the most senior people – it will be a matter of trust that the coach and individual are doing useful and effective work, and the sponsoring organisation will be happy to take a step back. In fact, this

"Sometimes senior leaders want to use extended external coaching as a stimulus to deeper reflection about the firm or their role, or as a catalyst to think 'outside the box'."

may be very important (even imperative) to some individuals being coached. In other cases, the business will want closer involvement in monitoring the outputs and results of the coaching, and the individual being coached will readily welcome this. Bearing in mind the need for flexibility, here are some possible approaches where a more rigorous approach is appropriate.

(a) Ensure that the coaching is aligned to business needs

A three or four-way discussion at the outset can ensure that there is alignment between:

- the individual;
- the coach;
- the organisation/budget holder (eg, HR); and
- the business sponsor (eg, the head of department or senior manager).

Although the individual and the coach will be the people who physically attend the coaching session, the interests of these three or four parties need to be taken into account. Areas that might be relevant for such briefings might include:

- the strategic objectives of the business or the relevant part of it;
- the culture and values to be reinforced; and
- the leadership behaviours expected (and currently being displayed).

(b) Agree measurable objectives at the outset

For example, write a business plan and establish a clear evaluation process. Evaluation should start from the moment that the coaching begins. Increasingly, organisations are using three or four-way contracting as above for coaching interventions to clarify their desired outcomes and success measures.

Sometimes senior leaders want to use extended external coaching as a stimulus to deeper reflection about the firm or their role, or as a catalyst to think 'outside the box'. In such case, it might be difficult to identify specific outputs, although "Generating more imaginative ideas about the future of the firm/Deciding how we should tackle X" might fit the bill. In any event, there needs to be some substantive answer to the question "Why is this coaching happening?" so that it is not, in effect, just a perk or a status symbol.

(c) Set a budget

Set a budget of, say, three meetings, and have a review before proceeding with any further coaching.

"Through the coaching process, coaches can develop a deep understanding of the firm's leadership behaviour and culture."

(d) Encourage all stakeholders to assess continuously whether progress is being made

HR (or L&D) and the business sponsor might provide ongoing support to the individual between coaching sessions. These meetings will encourage communication from the individual about how the coaching is going.

(e) Provide updates on progress to the budget holder or business sponsor

We would suggest that the individual provide this report; if the coach were to report, this would risk compromising the important boundary of trust between the individual and the coach.

(f) Harvest the learning from coaching

Through the coaching process, coaches can develop a deep understanding of the firm's leadership behaviour and culture. Panellists at a CIPD Coaching at Work conference agreed that it is acceptable to harvest data from coaches on organisational themes. However, this must be done with due concern for the individual's confidentiality, and must be for constructive organisational feedback and never for punitive measures.

1.7 Using coaching techniques in your everyday work

Coaching techniques – whether you have developed them yourself or seen them used by others – can be used as part of your day-to-day work. There are a number of models available – you can find many of these in books such as *The Little Book of Big Coaching Models*.[16] One that we particularly like – which you can adopt in meetings, for coaching and in your everyday life – is Nancy Kline's Thinking Environment. You can find out more from her website www.timetothink.com. Her Ten Components of a Thinking Environment are very useful tools, both in your role as a GC and in how you work with your team. They are:

> ***Attention*** *Listening without interruption and with interest in where the person will go next in their thinking.*
>
> ***Equality*** *Regarding each other as thinking peers giving equal time to think.*
>
> ***Ease*** *Discarding internal urgency.*
>
> ***Appreciation*** *Noticing what is good and saying it.*
>
> ***Feelings*** *Welcoming the release of emotion.*
>
> ***Encouragement*** *Giving courage to go to the unexplored edge of our thinking by ceasing competition as thinkers.*
>
> ***Information*** *Supplying facts, recognizing social context, dismantling denial.*
>
> ***Difference*** *Championing our inherent diversity of identity and thought.*
>
> ***Incisive*** *Questions Freeing the human mind of an untrue assumption lived as true.*
>
> ***Place*** *Producing a physical environment – the room, the listener, your body that says 'You matter'.*[17]

Also useful is Neil's Wheel (www.neilswheel.org) – a free tool for professional coaches and clients to help promote deeper, inspiring and transformative conversations allowing you to discuss the various components of your (and your team's) life, aspirations and objectives.

Tip: Actively seek out some useful coaching techniques for you and your team.

2. Mentoring

As discussed above, the key difference between coaching and mentoring is that the mentor can also share role or sector-specific knowledge with the mentee. Paul Gilbert of LBC Wise Counsel defines 'mentoring' as follows:

> *a confidential, respectful, non-judgemental conversation to explore issues and ideas of the moment as well as to help individuals develop their skills and their potential as an in-house lawyer. Most of our mentors have been senior in-house lawyers, but we also have mentors with different career/life experiences. Although there is a lot of debate about the differences between coaching and mentoring we make the distinction that coaches should be formally qualified as coaches, follow a recognised methodology and be judged against specific outcomes. Mentoring however is less formal, offering senior and experienced peer support albeit in a structured way.*[18]

You may decide to act as a mentor to your team, but really this is more like line management rather than true mentoring. Having someone – a former GC, for example – who can act as your mentor and talk through issues that they have also have faced in their career can be enormously valuable. Indeed, we believe that having a few close mentors throughout your career will help considerably with your progress – it has certainly helped us. So while having someone with a similar background as a mentor can be very helpful, it can also be useful to have someone as a mentor who has a different background. One of us has a former CFO and now serial non-executive director (NED) as a valued mentor. Some companies encourage mentoring from employees elsewhere in the business and this can be very useful. However, having someone external, perhaps throughout your career, can be very beneficial too,

So what might you decide to have mentoring for? Experienced mentor Paul Gilbert has identified a number of reasons for mentoring:

- *Personal career development*
- *Whether and when to move in-house*
- *Handling difficult relationship issues in the workplace*
- *Developing your leadership credentials*
- *Developing your management credentials*
- *Personal effectiveness*
- *Managing time and priorities*
- *Articulating your value*
- *Becoming more comfortable with finance as part of developing business acumen*
- *Project planning*

- *Your next move*
- *Handling a career gap*
- *Returning after a break*
- *Moving into a non-legal role*
- *Aspiring to lead in a non-legal role.*[19]

We hope that this chapter has given you some useful insights into managing your team, coaching and mentoring – all of which should help you to secure your reputation in the business. Talking of which...

VIII. The GC and the board

I have a special practice. I handle one client. Now you have my number, I'll await your call.[20]

1. Background to your board relationship

If, as the GC, you have interaction with the board, then like Tom Hagan in *The Godfather*, you will need to await their call and be ready to respond when you receive it. Quickly! One of us in his GC role spent about half his time working with the board on board-related matters, and the role tends to take precedence over everything else. You will need to prioritise the board over anything else you do, and that can cause frustrations with other people in the business.

Don't naturally assume, however, that you will always be at board meetings – unless you wear the company secretary hat, in which case you will be there to act in that capacity (more about this later on). But it is very rare indeed for the GC to sit on the board as a full member – only a tiny proportion of GCs ever do this. In part, that is because the role is seen by many boards as an advisory function; but there is also an independence issue: can you really act as an independent, objective adviser if you are also a member of the body you are advising? So if, as the GC, you are ever asked to sit on the board, that is something to think carefully about before agreeing. In our view, you are better placed in the role of independent adviser than full board member.

"If, as the GC, you are ever asked to sit on the board, that is something to think carefully about before agreeing. In our view, you are better placed in the role of independent adviser than full board member."

Another reason why you may not attend board meetings is simply due to a limit on the number of attendees. A common complaint of boards – especially from NEDs – is that the more people who attend, the more this tends to curtail the room for debate and discussion, and extend the meeting. Accordingly, the chair may only want key decision makers and advisers present. You may regard yourself as fitting into this category – and in many ways, you do – but the board can always communicate their needs to you or ask you to attend when they believe your advice or counsel is required. While this is not ideal – there may be occasions when the board are unaware that legal advice is necessary or that a legal issue has arisen – boards (like everything else) are not perfect. One way to ensure that you have a good feel for what is going on is to foster your relationship with the CEO or the company secretary, who may have a reporting line to you in any event. And you can always ask to see the minutes and pick up any issues from there.

In addition, while attending the board meetings may seem important and interesting – after all, it allows you to find out what is going on at the top of the company – you may need to assess how much of a priority this really is. If you are heading a sizeable legal team, you will have the flexibility to spend time at board and board committee meetings (which may take a fair chunk of time); but if you are a sole

GC in the business, you may need to assess what is most important to ensure that the company is fully and effectively serviced from a legal standpoint. That said, in heavily regulated sectors, it is likely that the GC will attend board meetings whether or not they have the time!

Whatever your time with and exposure to the board, this is a very important part of your role; so how do you make the relationship a successful one?

2. Build your relationship with the board with care

In its seminal report, *Do You Have the Right C-Suite?*,[21] Heidrick & Struggles states that: "For the General Counsel, who must have a strong working relationship with the CEO but whose client is ultimately the company... expectations require a delicate balancing act as well as a wide range of leadership abilities."

Tip: Understand how boards work and build your relationship with your board with care. Humility and being on top of your brief are key.

There is no doubt that this is a role that requires both diplomacy and independence. Building an effective relationship takes time and careful nurturing; destroying it is quicker and easier. So, how best to build it?

- Stay on top of your brief – always! In your interactions with the board, they will require your counsel and guidance; but for them to put their trust in you, they will also require confidence in your abilities and effectiveness. One of us earlier in his career recalls the chair turning around and saying, "I look to you as general counsel to keep me and the other members of the board out of prison." He was only half joking and in any event this was an area where we outperformed! But seriously, when a member of the board turns to you, you must be able to provide an answer – or at least give an initial view and know where to get a firm response and by when.
- Boards don't generally like lawyers and they like the law even less! While this may seem an exaggeration – in respect of lawyers at least – it is often not far from the truth. Lawyers are frequently seen as problem causers and expensive. If you are asked to advise on a matter, do just that, but don't bore the board with the law – they are simply not interested. They want a solution to their issue – either from you or outsourced.
- But they do want an answer. In this respect, you must treat the board like anyone else you advise. The law is complex and full of shades of grey – directors appreciate that. But they need an answer, and one of the great benefits you have over external lawyers is having a better idea of the context – for example, the

company you work for and the board members – as well as not having to cover your back with caveats. One of us advises boards frequently and a common feature he has noticed is that the two principal skills that directors need are courage and integrity. Most have the latter; many fewer have the former. The same is true for lawyers: you must give a view. One of the directors we spoke to said he found that the best GCs working at board level were those who outlined a straightforward answer to a particular risk and assessed on a percentage basis the chances of it occurring, as well as the best practical ways to deal with all of its aspects.

- If you do make a mistake, own up. We all make mistakes and everyone will respect you the more for it. One of us once forgot to do something for a board meeting and had the dilemma of hoping that the matter would go away or brushing over it. He chose the latter; two of the directors rolled their eyes and he felt foolish. But at least he had been open. Years later, one of the eye-rolling directors told him how much he had admired this honesty, and that when the director himself had been less transparent with another board he was on, it had ended in disaster. Remember: once the board no longer trusts you, you have no place as their adviser.

"Wear your intellect lightly, but your gravitas highly. You need to look and act the part at all times."

- Wear your intellect lightly, but your gravitas highly. You need to look and act the part at all times. Again, it is all about instilling confidence. One GC we know – a very bright individual – has a habit of cracking jokes to the board, as well as other people he advises. Believe us, if the board want some light relief, there are other means available. While the board don't want a po-faced GC, they wouldn't dream of taking legal advice from a regular performer at the Comedy Store, so you shouldn't act in that way either. Be serious but approachable in your dealings with the board, even if they scare the hell out of you (they shouldn't).
- You should be the board's 'extra conscience'. As Patrick Dunne writes about the GC (and company secretary) in his book *Boards: A Practical Perspective*:[22] "The best act as the board's extra conscience and confidant to every member. They will also play a central role in ensuring that relations between the board and the executive are effective."
- It is important to be able to fulfil these roles, as well as acting as an independent and objective adviser to the board. However, this can be a challenge to balance in practice. Your role, as GC at least, will report to the CEO or maybe the CFO. While you need to have a relationship with the board, you need to manage your relationship with the CEO first and foremost, unless very exceptional circumstances arise. However good and close your relationship is with the board, you will never be the principal (executive) player – that position very much rests with the CEO. So ensuring that the CEO is not taken unduly by surprise by what you are talking about at board meetings will strengthen your relationship with them (they are, after all, a very important component of the board), make you more effective and, of course, ensure your longevity. You should let the CEO run the main relationship with the board and be the major player – so big news should come from them. CEOs are often people with large egos, to whom humility is an alien concept; so even if the CEO ventures into your area of responsibility and speaks on your behalf (a common occurrence), it is probably best to let this go – you can always add your own contribution to what they have said. All of this doesn't mean, of course, that you should be afraid to speak up when necessary; and in extreme cases, you may have to talk to the chair or other board members about and without the CEO if there is any hint of unethical behaviour. Hopefully, however, this will be the exception rather than the rule.
- Don't be afraid to speak up, but be clear on the mandate. As we have outlined above, you should be able to add your contribution. But just as the CEO may hog the conversation and cover all the areas of their direct reports, this is something you should never do. As one GC we spoke to advised, it is fine to talk

outside your area (to an extent) at exco level; but at the board, stick to your brief – literally. That is what you are there for and what the board wants you to opine on – as we have written elsewhere, as much as you might want to give a view on corporate strategy, it's best to leave that to the experts. At least one of the GCs we spoke to generally left it to the chair and CEO to bring him in when they felt this was necessary – he had built up a sufficiently good relationship with them that he knew they would call him in when needed. That said, you should be well known to the board and be prepared to speak up when required. Having evaluated boards, we have seen instances where the GC simply sits throughout the whole meeting and says little or nothing; you do need to contribute, at the very least when asked.

- Get to know how boards work. We will examine this more fully in the next chapter, but suffice to say here that if you have not worked with boards before, seek to understand how they function from an overall governance, structural and dynamics view. A listed public limited company (PLC) board with both executives and non-executives will be very different from the board of a private company, a charity or a non-governmental organisation. You need to understand the dynamics.
- And the politics! All boards have political undercurrents – some members who get on well, others less so. You could be unlucky and join a board where the two most important members – the chair and CEO – do not get on and there is a good deal of conflict and tension. If this is the case, your powers of discretion and diplomacy may come to the fore; but being the GC to a dysfunctional board can be very lonely and frustrating. This may be where having a mentor or coach becomes important.
- While the board is at the apex of any business, remember that it is also a team, and in this respect it shares many of the features of other teams within the business. Therefore, treat it in this way too. Show the value that you can add – not least in reducing costs and being able to provide immediate and contextual legal advice in a way that an external lawyer may be unable to. Equally, don't be offended if the board wants a second opinion from an external source on a material matter. You cannot be an expert in everything and, in any event, you are likely to be the person deciphering the advice to make it more manageable for the board. As you will know as an experienced GC, the ability to determine when to do something yourself and when to outsource is critical to your effectiveness and the success of the organisation.
- Recognise the conflicts. Boards are full of conflicts. Many are legal and corporate conflicts, but there are others too. However, one conflict you must remember is your own. In essence, your

"You need to remember that you are an adviser to the company first and foremost. There will be situations where the directors need advice, but you cannot advise them, as that would conflict with your duty to the company."

client is the company. The interests of the company and the directors will normally coincide; but on rare occasions, they may not. This is when you need to remember that you are an adviser to the company first and foremost. There will be situations where the directors need advice, but you cannot advise them, as that would conflict with your duty to the company. A company going into a type of insolvency may be an example. Recognise this and, more importantly, have a recommended panel of external legal advisers for the board (different from your company panel, of course), to whom the directors can turn. You need this to hand because when this type of situation arises, external legal advice may be needed very quickly indeed.

- Finally, when you work with boards as the GC, remember that although this can be both stressful and frustrating, it is also an immense privilege. You will be working with the people who determine where the company is going (or not going!), and witness their hopes, fears, objectives and foibles. However, with privilege comes responsibility. Much of what goes on at the board will be confidential and needs to remain so. This is even more the case with listed companies. It goes without saying that the board will expect you to respect the confidential nature of what they do.

IX. Taking on the role of company secretary

As the great ones depart, eating their dinner, the secretary sits getting thinner and thinner, racking his brain as he tries to record and report what he thinks they think they ought to have thought.[23]

We wouldn't suggest that you take the above quote as a recommendation not to take on the role of company secretary – although if you do, you may find that there is a grain of truth in it. This will all depend on the board that you are dealt, of course!

1. A bit of background

We are assuming that most people reading this book will take on the role of company secretary in addition to their position as GC. But of course, it is quite possible to undertake this role on its own – it has become a much more popular career choice for lawyers; and indeed, in many companies, such as major listed ones, there is a good argument that the role should be separate and distinct from that of the GC.

The company secretary is an officer of the company, just as the directors are. While there is no longer a strict requirement for a private company in the United Kingdom to have a company secretary (subject to some exceptions), public limited companies – both listed and unlisted – must have one. This person must have certain qualifications – barrister and solicitor are just two of the professions that meet the requirements – although there is scope for the board to widen the scope of the appointment if certain conditions aren't met. To find out more about the legal requirements for the role, we would recommend looking at *The ICSA Company Secretary's Handbook*,[24] which provides more background. Here, we are much more interested in the dynamic and operational aspects of the position of company secretary.

So, what do you need to do before you take it on?

2. Understand the nature of the role

One of the best descriptions of the role of company secretary is set out in the Financial Reporting Council's *Guidance on Board Effectiveness*.[25] This guide is also a helpful publication if you want to understand boards generally, their structure and dynamics, and how they work or should work. While the guidance is aimed principally at listed companies (as with the UK Corporate Governance Code), many other companies follow it and much of it is applicable to other organisations. You can read the full description of the company secretary's role in paragraphs 79–84, but briefly, the role encompasses the following:

> *79. The company secretary is responsible for ensuring that board procedures are complied with, advising the board on all governance matters, supporting the chair and helping the board and its committees to function efficiently..*
>
> *81. Under the direction of the chair, the company secretary's responsibilities include ensuring good information flows within the board and its committees and between senior management and non-executive directors, as well as facilitating induction, arranging board training and assisting with professional development as required...*
>
> *83. It is the responsibility of the company secretary to ensure that directors, especially non-executive directors, have access to independent professional advice at the company's expense where they judge it necessary to discharge their responsibilities as directors of the company...*
>
> *84. Assisting the chair in establishing the policies and processes the board needs in order to function properly is a core part of the company secretary's role...*
>
> *85. The company secretary's effectiveness can be enhanced by building relationships of mutual trust with the chair, the senior independent director and the non-executive directors, while maintaining the confidence of executive director colleagues. They are in a unique position between the executive and the board...*[26]

This last point is especially important. An effective company secretary is an important component of a well-performing board – so if you take away nothing else from this chapter, be sure not to underrate the importance of the role or see it merely as a bolt-on to the GC position.

One of the biggest challenges with the company secretary role – and what may differentiate it from that of the GC – is the need to build good relationships with the most senior people in the company: the directors. This is more challenging than might at first appear. Often, the company secretary will be the only other person in a board meeting with the directors. Yet while they are all equal to each other, the company secretary is not on the same level (very few company secretaries are also directors and – for the reasons outlined in the previous chapter about the need for the independence of the GC – nor should they be). Good people skills and the ability to deal with stressful situations are absolutely essential.

Another challenge – and one that you cannot easily address before taking on the role – is that nearly every board sees the role of the company secretary in a slightly different way. We have seen this in the board evaluation work we do, with even the same chair viewing the company secretaries of the various boards she chairs in a different

"An effective company secretary is an important component of a well-performing board... be sure not to underrate the importance of the role or see it merely as a bolt-on to the GC position."

"While influencing skills will always be of importance as a GC, they are even more so in the boardroom, given that you will be among a group of equals, but not part of that equality yourself."

light. Navigating this can be tricky and you need to ensure that the role works for you as well as for the board.

The complexity and ranges of the role of the company secretary are perhaps best illustrated by an interesting assessment by McNulty and Stewart:

> *1. Humble clerk: the company secretary has responsibility for statutory returns and regulatory compliance;*
>
> *2. Chair support: the chair's aide de camp as he or she operates the board with the support of the company secretary;*
>
> *3. Advocate for the collective conscience of the company: the secretary, as a unique legal officer of the company, distinct from that of a director, can steer the board to exercise a collective conscience;*
>
> *4. Boundary spanner: occupying an independent position, between the executive and the non-executive, the role affords the company secretary brokerage opportunities as the go-between;*
>
> *5. Honest broker: the company secretary can engage in activities,*

to manage information flows, and broker effective and meaningful relationships between other members of the board; and

6. Governance change agent: the secretary can directly and/or indirectly influence board process and outcomes.[27]

We think you should aim to fulfil roles 2 to 6, but you may have at times to fulfil the first one too. However, roles 2 and 6 are vital components if you are going to succeed in the role; and while influencing skills will always be of importance as a GC, they are even more so in the boardroom, given that you will be among a group of equals, but not part of that equality yourself. This means that using your EQ skills and influencing will be critical to your success.

Tip: If you are going to take on the company secretary role, talk to some people who are currently in that role and ask them for their tips on fulfilling it successfully.

If you are asked – or required – to take on the role, sit down with the chair early on to find out what they expect, how they see your role playing out and what help they will need in running the board. Talk to a few seasoned company secretaries about how they have undertaken the role and the pitfalls; and see whether one of them will be a mentor to you on the board.

In your role as company secretary, it is quite common for you to report to the chair, given that you are helping them to run the board (which is quite different from running the organisation itself). You also need to discuss the role with your CEO (if they are the person you report to) and how it will work in practice. You need to be clear on reporting lines when you are wearing the hat of the company secretary, because you may be placed in situations of conflict. For example, it is quite common with a unitary board (see below) for the NEDs to meet alone without the executives present; but they may ask the company secretary to remain, in order to advise and take the minutes. These sessions are usually confidential and discussion may take place about the senior executives, including the CEO. This can place you in a difficult situation, because you will be privy to views and opinions about your boss, but must maintain the confidence of the boardroom session. So be aware! Or beware!

3. Get an understanding of boards if you don't already have one

It is likely that you will have had interaction with boards while working your way up to become GC. However, your exposure to them may have been fleeting; so if you do take on the role of company secretary, it is worth getting to know how boards in different structures work. For example, if you are company secretary to a listed PLC, you will be working with a unitary board made up of both executive directors and NEDs; while a smaller private company may only have executive directors and will be very different in nature. Again, to gain an understanding of the different roles, the Financial Reporting Council's Guidance on Board Effectiveness is a good resource. Below is a brief description of each of the roles from the guidance:

> ***Chair***
> *The chair is pivotal in creating the conditions for overall board and individual director effectiveness, setting clear expectations concerning the style and tone of board discussions, ensuring the board has effective decision-making processes and applies sufficient challenge to major proposals.*
>
> ***Senior independent director***
> *The senior independent director should act as a sounding board for the chair, providing them with support in the delivery of their objectives and leading the evaluation of the chair on behalf of the other directors.*
>
> ***Non-executive directors***
> *It is vital that non-executive directors have sufficient time available to discharge their responsibilities effectively. The time commitment to engage with shareholders and other key stakeholders and get to know the business can be considerable.*
>
> ***Executive directors***
> *Executive directors have the same duties as other members of a unitary board. These duties extend to the whole of the business, and not just that part of it covered by their individual executive roles.*[28]

Case study: a life in the day of a company secretary
We interviewed a GC who now undertakes the company secretary role to find out more about what it involves.

How did your company secretary role come about?
It was a bit of a leap in the dark, but I had worked with the previous company secretary – the role looked interesting and I was asked to take it on. Having a handover was very useful, but it is very different from the normal GC role.

Should the GC/company secretary role be split?
Yes, unless there is huge support. I now do very little legal work and need to focus on the company secretarial side. That said, I don't really miss the day-to-day legal work, as I still get involved – just at a higher level.

What are your tips for taking on the role?

- Be clear on what the responsibilities are.
- You cannot just bolt this on to the GC role and you need to be very clear on the split between the two roles if you do both (although this is not recommended). You also need to clarify what support you will need and this may differ throughout the year.

What skills and attributes do you need?

- Good interpersonal skills;
- An excellent relationship with the chair and with the NEDs in general, and a full understanding of their needs;
- The confidence and ability to speak up;
- Gravitas;
- Courage on opinions or advice; and
- Discretion – according to my CEO, this is the most important quality that the company secretary brings to the table, and I think that is right. You also need to be a good diplomat.

In building your relationship with the chair, you will need to recognise that different chairs have different priorities. Also, sometimes it can be difficult to advise the chair, given your executive responsibilities; and it can also be difficult to arrange private meetings with the NEDs.

The challenges of the role include the following:

- **Staying on top of things:** This relates not only to the admin (eg, papers and minutes need to be circulated on time), but also to the governance side – you need to keep 100% up to date here, as the NEDs will be relying on you for governance advice.
- **Listed companies:** The role of company secretary is a very different beast if the company is listed. The burden is huge and growing, and I often feel that it's impossible to stay ahead. Reporting and accounts are huge processes which are very time consuming. Section 172 stakeholder reporting is also a major issue to address; as are the changes to the UK Corporate Governance Code.
- **Administration of meetings:** This involves huge amounts of preparation, as I am the key point of contact. You may find yourself having to arrange lunch, so don't be too precious! You will also be responsible for the IT side of the meeting, so you need good IT support. Test the systems before the meeting and check them yourself.
- **Diversity of the role:** You will have to advise on many issues and won't always get validation.

We also spoke to someone who had moved from private practice to a media organisation which had an unusual (although perhaps not unique) structure: a charitable body with a board of (high-profile) trustees oversaw a corporate business with its own board. He was company secretary to the charity, while the corporate business had a separate legal department and a head of legal. Not surprisingly, his main message concerned the need to be politically and personally sensitive to this varied range of stakeholders.

X. What next? Reinventing yourself

1. The importance of thinking ahead

John Cleese, Jerry Springer, Fidel Castro, Henri Matisse and Andrea Bocelli – all very different people, but with one thing in common: they either were or started out training to be lawyers, before branching out into different careers. Now, not everyone can be the next Matisse or Bocelli; but you should constantly review your career and where it is going, together with your longer-term objectives. In the early days of our careers, often spurred on by 'vaulting ambition', we tend to think only of an upwards trajectory. But careers aren't really like that and generally involve highs and lows – and hopefully highs again. More than that, the world is changing – 2020 has brought that point home to all of us perhaps more than anything else could; and while your role as a GC in a particular sector may be in demand today, tomorrow both you and it may be history.

It is important, therefore, to think ahead in career terms, even if you are really enjoying your job and believe that it will last for ever. Some great insight on the world of work can be gleaned from management guru Charles Handy, as one of us wrote elsewhere in relation to his book *The Second Curve: Thoughts on Reinventing Society*:[29]

> [The Second Curve] *is the principle that you should change before you hit a peak as it is much harder to do so once you are on a*

downward spiral. Handy is a prime example – he has been an executive, academic, consultant and author always changing at the right time or just before. The book contains some scary facts for all of us: for example, the prediction that half of all the jobs today will cease to exist in just 15 years; by 2035 47% of all roles will be performed by computer. Oh that's just another wild prediction you say. Well not really. It is happening now. To illustrate the point: the big corporations that employed thousands of people are changing – for example, while a big company like Kodak employed 145,000 people an even 'bigger' organisation like Facebook employs just 6,000. The definition of what means 'big' is changing – rapidly. Big no longer means lots of employees.

Lawyers – external and in-house – are not immune from this. Quite the reverse – as Handy rightly points out much basic legal work will be performed by computers in the future without the need for you and me. The legal world will be radically different in five years and possibly unrecognisable in fifteen. Yet we still train more and more lawyers. That wouldn't be so bad in itself but we are training them very much in our own image – to have the type of career we have had – the only one we have known. But legal careers in the future will be very different. We must create a new future for ourselves – we have to imagine what the new world will be like and create a place for ourselves in that new world. Those who survive are those who best adapt to change. We all need to be able to do this if we are to survive in this new world. However I wonder if adapting alone may now be enough – maybe we have to imagine and create that new life at the right time or just shortly before as Handy would tell us.

So what's your point? Very simply don't be afraid to imagine what the future will be like or to adapt. Try new things – whether that means working abroad or going on secondment to a department other than the legal one. Maybe you will return to Legal, maybe you won't. But you'll be more easily able to adapt to change and to imagine or create your future. Timing is of course everything and knowing when the second curve has arrived is a challenge. However, keep an open mind – both in business and in life – and maybe you will reach it. Sometimes at least![30]

2. Re-evaluating your career

As we have highlighted above, it is important to keep your career as a GC under review. Perhaps your first choice is to decide whether you want to continue in your legal role. Many lawyers do and would not dream of doing anything else. For others, the path is less clear-cut. However, even if you do wish to continue, it is prudent to take a sense check from time to time as to how realistic this is. As companies become more reliant on technologies such as artificial intelligence, there may be a reduction in the number of employees they need, as outlined in the passage above – the advice in the last paragraph is particularly important.

3. Staying in a legal role

If you do want to continue in a GC role, then acquiring new skills or taking on new responsibilities may broaden your interests and experience, as well as bolstering your career in the face of future challenges. Some GCs take on the company secretary position, as outlined in the previous chapter, which opens up the world of corporate governance and opportunities to work with the highest echelons of management. Others may follow the example of Simon Cox outlined in Chapter II and take responsibility for other functions, such as HR – although, as he advises, it is important to have the right level of support to do so successfully. Another option may be to work more closely as an adviser to the CEO – the *consigliere* to whom they turn at times of both crisis and opportunity. In this way, you can build your degree of influence and value. If you are clear that you want to remain in the role of GC, that's fine; but make sure that you develop the role and you yourself develop – it is all about learning.

"If you do want to continue in a GC role, then acquiring new skills or taking on new responsibilities may broaden your interests and experience, as well as bolstering your career in the face of future challenges."

4. Moving away from the GC role

So, what if you are done with being GC? Some very sage advice comes from another business guru, Peter Drucker. In his seminal work, *Managing Oneself*,[31] Drucker writes:

> *Knowledge workers, therefore, face drastically new demands:*
>
> *1. They have to ask: Who Am I? What are My Strengths? How Do I Work?*
>
> *2. They have to ask: Where Do I Belong?*
>
> *3. They have to ask: What is My Contribution?*
>
> *4. They have to take Relationship Responsibility*
>
> *5. They have to plan for the Second Half of their Lives*

This is an excellent framework both for those planning a new career and for those who intend to continue in the same role. Asking and answering these questions may help you to identify some alternative career paths. The framework can also be used with a careers coach.

"Don't underestimate the challenge of changing careers ... it can take time, determination and setbacks before achieving success; and of course, that is never guaranteed."

Don't underestimate the challenge of changing careers, however: it can take time, determination and setbacks before achieving success; and of course, that is never guaranteed. However, many of those moving away from the GC role do because they have a particular interest that they wish to explore. Perhaps they want to work in a business role and get closer to the commercial action. Or maybe they want to forge a different career path altogether: to become a consultant, perhaps, or even do something completely unrelated to law or business – remember Matisse!

5. Moving to a new career

If, as a GC, you are thinking along these lines, it may because it accords with what Drucker says in his final point, on thinking about the second half of your life:

> *One can no longer expect that the organization for which one works at age thirty will still be around when one reaches age sixty. But also, forty or fifty in the same kind of work is much too long for most people. They deteriorate, get bored, lose all joy in their work, "retire on the job" and become a burden to themselves and to everyone around them.*[32]

While this may perhaps be a little harsh, it is valuable to recognise that as your life changes, your career aspirations do too. One of us recalls a colleague saying that once he had passed the age of 40, his career ambitions fell off a cliff. Of course, it needn't be like this; and nor should it be. There are plenty of options. Both of us transitioned from the law into careers as consultants with wide-ranging practices. While this has not always been without challenge, it has been an amazing journey, allowing us to meet people and have experiences that we would never have done otherwise. But don't just take our word for it – below, three lawyers share their thoughts and experiences from their diverse careers.

5.1 Louisa Elder – lawyer turned coach

Louisa Elder (www.louisaelder.com) was a private practice lawyer who undertook a number of in-house secondments She then worked for one of the big consultancy practices as chief of staff. She now works as a coach, mainly with legal sector clients.

What was it like being chief of staff?

It was an incredible experience – like doing an MBA. I saw many different areas, so there was valuable learning; but you need to be able to think quickly on your feet. But lots of your legal skills are transferable ones – never forget that.

Chief of staff is a good role for lawyers, but it's not one where you get bogged down in the detail – so it may suit some more than others.

Why did you leave the law?
I thought about what I have enjoyed in my career – mentoring and coaching – and wanted to adapt that into a new challenge and a new career.

Coaching can be very inspiring, but you need to listen in an active way and ask powerful questions. Strong intuition is also an advantage.

What advice would you give those starting out in new careers?

- Remain true to your values and instinct.
- Don't be afraid of new challenges.
- Always remember that during uncomfortable times, growth happens. Don't always play it safe and secure – make an effort to go outside your comfort zone.

5.2 Paul Gilbert – founder and CEO of LBC Wise Counsel (www.lbcwisecounsel.com)

Why did you move in-house?
It wasn't a strategic plan, but I didn't see myself as a law firm partner. I had enjoyed working with a local finance company, helping to structure a deal with common sense. I saw an in-house role in the financial services sector and went for it. Once there, I loved it – I really got that area of law under my belt.

What advice would you give to a new GC?

- If you make a major decision in the first 100 days, it will probably be the wrong one. The key things to do are to listen, absorb and understand the business.
- In respect of your role, it is very easy to think you are everyone's best friend and that you will be able to do everything; but if you do, you will soon burn out, so you need to know your purpose.
- You will succeed or fail on the quality of your relationships, so focus on these, rather than on activity.

Why did you move outside the law?
I loved being an in-house lawyer, but I had two reasons for leaving. First, I was a GC quite young and I hadn't really learned enough for that level of responsibility. Second, I moved into another GC role when my company was taken over and I didn't really know the people or the company well enough.

I felt vulnerable in both roles and realised that these types of roles need support – a go-to person for GCs – so I thought about it for six months and then went for it. I gave it a year to see if I could make a success of it. Though it was a brave decision, a braver one was to continue after three or four years, when it was no longer possible to go back.

What advice would you give someone who wants to move on from the role of GC?

- Have the right attitude!
- Either do it or don't – it's not a small thing! You can't trade on previous GC roles for long, as you need to stay current and relevant.

What would you do differently?

Nothing – it's been an amazing adventure. I would have been better off financially if I had stuck to being a GC, but it would not have been the same. I've had the opportunity to travel and meet hundreds of lawyers around the world – it's been an amazing privilege.

What advice would you give the young Paul Gilbert?

- Careers are not linear and predictable.
- Be adventurous as far as your tolerance to change allows.
- If you have to move backwards or sideways, then do so.
- No day is wasted if you are thoughtful about the experience.
- Understand the difference you can make.

5.3 Claire Carless – former GC at St Andrew's Healthcare

Being a GC involves a broad range of experience and skills – the clue, as they say, is in the title. So in my view, getting experience outside the GC role is vital, to help develop different perspectives and to bring a balance and some pragmatism to the role. I've been fortunate to hold a number of non-executive and trustee roles, including with the South Central Ambulance Service, the Oxford University Audit and Scrutiny Committee and Home-Start West Berkshire, which have not only given me an outside interest, but also helped me to develop skills that I have been able to bring to my GC roles. There's nothing better than being a NED to help you understand what NEDs look for and need from a GC.

The last six months have given me other opportunities. At the start of the pandemic, I was asked to take on the interim manager role at St Andrew's Hospital in Birmingham, before the permanent appointee was able to start. The hospital looks after around 120 patients who are detained under the Mental Health Act, and COVID-19 added a whole new set of challenges to what was already a complex and demanding hospital environment. It was a tough gig, but I have no doubt that the skills I've learned as a GC helped me through it – remaining calm in a crisis, considering the issues carefully and then making thoughtful and balanced decisions, and communicating them clearly.

And now I've started a long-planned 'gap year' with my husband, volunteering and travelling around the world. I'm writing this from Jamaica, where we're starting our journey, working on a range of projects, from videos for pre-school children to helping a rum business apply for a grant for new machinery. It's a short stop in my career (relatively speaking), but one that I'm sure will give me more rich experiences that will enhance my role as GC wherever I land on my return.

5.4 The role of the NED

Claire's insights from her experiences as a NED lead us to another question that we frequently get asked by lawyers, both in-house and in private practice: how to become a NED. These roles are highly sought after, even though the responsibility and liability have increased in recent years.

So, here are a few final tips for those considering this move:

- Don't underestimate the scale of the challenge in securing a NED role – particularly a paid one. While legal skills are highly transferable and useful around the boardroom table, they are not the skills in most demand. Few lawyers have run commercial enterprises and this is often the background that boards look for in NEDS.
- That said, legal skills can be very useful, particularly in highly regulated industries such as financial services, so these types of sectors are useful to target.
- One way to start is to undertake a trustee role first, for a charity or not-for-profit. That will give you good boardroom experience.
- Emphasise your governance and boardroom skills if you have been the company secretary.
- The time commitment can be high. If you are also doing a GC role – or have another executive position – you will need to bear in mind how to balance the two. However difficult it might be, if the organisation you are on the board of finds itself in a crisis, that will have to be the priority, as you have personal liability. This can be difficult to explain to your CEO! Many NEDs that we have come across really underestimated the commitment, because they didn't take into account the fact that the time involved increases three or fourfold when the company is in crisis.

So whether you decide to remain in your GC role or move to something new, good luck – and make sure it is an interesting journey!

Endnotes

1 Mario Puzo and Francis Ford Coppola, *The Godfather* (screenplay) (1972).
2 Brene Brown, *The Gifts of Imperfection* (Vermilion, 2020).
3 David Lagercrantz, *The Girl in the Spider's Web* (Norstedts Forlag, 2015). Partially referred to in an article, *The Critical Role of the GC in Governance, Risk and Compliance* by Ian White for Wolters Kluwer, 2016.
4 Heidrick & Struggles International, *Do You Have the Right C-Suite? Tough Questions CEOs Today Are Asking* (2013), p15.
5 *Ibid*, p17.
6 See the work of Arie de Geus, author of *The Living Company* (1997) and an expert on scenario planning.
7 Lowell Bryan, "Enduring Ideas: The 7-S Framework", *McKinsey Quarterly*, 1 March 2008.
8 Peter Honey and Alan Mumford, *The Manual of Learning Styles* (Peter Honey Publications, 1982).
9 David Nadler, "Building Better Boards", *Harvard Business Review*, May 2004, p3.
10 Lewis Carroll, *Alice's Adventures in Wonderland* (Macmillan, 1865).
11 Presentation made at LBC Wise Counsel Cambridge Conference.
12 Ian White, "The Law Department of Today and Why it Needs to Change", in Alex Davies (ed), *Building the Law Department of Tomorrow* (Ark Group, 2017), p52.
13 Financial Reporting Council, *Corporate Culture and the Role of Boards* (2016), p2.
14 Paul Gilbert, *A Report on the Well Being of In-House Lawyers* (LBC Wise Counsel, 2015), p3.
15 White (n 12), p53.
16 Bob Bates, *The Little Book of Big Coaching Models* (Pearson, 2015).
17 Nancy Kline, *The Promise that Changes Everything: I won't Interrupt You* (Penguin Life, 2020), p35.
18 LBC Wise Counsel, www.lbcwisecounsel.com/lawyer-mentoring/#.X7-ZdS2cbOQ.
19 LBC Wise Counsel, www.lbcwisecounsel.com/lawyer-mentoring/#.X-C8lS2cbOQ.
20 Puzo and Ford Coppola (n 1).
21 Heidrick & Struggles International Inc (n 4), p17.
22 Patrick Dunne, *Boards: A Practical Perspective* (Governance Publishing and Information Services Limited, 2019), p47.
23 Quote thought to be from Arthur Bryant, cited in Jennifer Robertson, *The Role of the Company Secretary: Influence, Impact and Integrity* (Australian Institute of Company Directors, 2018), p1.
24 Douglas Armour, *The ICSA Company Secretary's Handbook*, 11th edition (ICSA Institute, 2016).
25 Financial Reporting Council, *Guidance on Board Effectiveness*, 2018, paras 79–84, www.frc.org.uk.
26 *Ibid*, emphasis added.
27 T McNulty and A Stewart (2015), "Developing the governance space: A study of the role and potential of the company secretary in and around the board of directors", *Organization Studies*, Vol 36, No 4, p521, cited in Robertson (n 23), p13.
28 Financial Reporting Council (n 25) pp18–22.
29 Charles Handy, *The Second Curve: Thoughts on Reinventing Society* (Penguin Random House, 2015).
30 Article by Ian White on the LBC Wise Counsel website.
www.lbcwisecounsel.com/resources/articles/article/turning-the-lights-out-a-guest-post-by-ian-white/#.X7-bAC2cbOQ.
31 Peter Drucker, *Management Challenges for the 21st Century* (Routledge, 2011), p164.
32 *Ibid.*

About the authors

Ian White
Consultant, Sherwood PSF Consulting
ian.white@sherwoodpsfconsulting.com

Ian White is a former chief legal officer and company secretary for both listed and private companies. While he has spent most of his career as a lawyer, he also has an MBA and has spent some time working as a strategy consultant.

Ian now works as a consultant, coach, trainer and facilitator. His previous in-house experience has led him to develop expertise in corporate governance, working with boards, leaders and lawyers on effectiveness, enhancement and performance. He spends much of his time reviewing and advising boards and management teams on structure, dynamics and how they can excel in leading their organisations. While his main focus is on FTSE 100/250 and major private companies, he also works with professional services firms, public sector bodies and a number of charities and other not-for-profit organisations.

Ian also helps lawyers, both in-house and in private practice, to work more closely and effectively with their clients, encouraging them to think of themselves as business people first and lawyers second.

Simon McCall
Director, Sherwood PSF Consulting Limited
simon.mccall@sherwoodpsfconsulting.com

Simon McCall is a management consultant and business coach. He works mainly with lawyers, in private practice and in-house. Over 30 years, his consulting assignments have included helping in-house departments to develop a compelling strategy and law firm management teams to work more effectively together. Simon has designed and led management development programmes for lawyers at associate and partner level. As a coach, Simon has enabled lawyers to explore and plan changes to how they work and how they build successful relationships with colleagues.

Simon has a law degree from the University of Cambridge and qualified as a solicitor in 1980 with Lawrence Graham. He then worked in-house with Houlder Offshore (an oil drilling business) and American Express. He has an MBA from the Cranfield School of Management. Simon was a principal tutor on the Nottingham Law School MBA in legal practice and did his coaching training with The School of Coaching.

About Globe Law and Business

Globe Law and Business was established in 2005. From the very beginning, we set out to create law books which are sufficiently high level to be of real use to the experienced professional, yet still accessible and easy to navigate. Most of our authors are drawn from Magic Circle and other top commercial firms, both in the UK and internationally.

Our titles are carefully produced, with the utmost attention paid to editorial, design and production processes. We hope this results in high-quality publications that are easy to read, and a pleasure to own. Our titles are also available as ebooks, which are compatible with most desktop, laptop and tablet devices. In 2018 we expanded our portfolio to include journals and Special Reports, available both digitally and in hard copy format, and produced to the same high standards as our books.

We'd very much like to hear from you with your thoughts and ideas for improving what we offer. Please do feel free to email me at sian@globelawandbusiness.com with your views.

Sian O'Neill
Managing director
Globe Law and Business
www.globelawandbusiness.com

Notes and ideas